INFORMATION TECHNOLOGY PERFORMANCE

JOE TEMPLE

FOREWORD

Early in my career, I took graduate classes in Systems and Computer Science at Union College extension in Poughkeepsie, NY. One of the classes was in the application of queueing theory to computer systems. This was my introduction to the analysis of computer and systems performance. For hardware design engineers, performance was always the fundamental objective, but we had little understanding of how the design requirements we were working toward were derived from actual work run by clients.

Over time as I moved from distributed processor to mainframe and then to supercomputer development, I became aware that the metrics changed, but the disconnect from the client view was still there. Later on, I found that the disconnect extended to the users of computers.

In the late 1990s, three types of computing (Distributed Computers, Mainframes, and Supercomputers) collided in the marketplace. I took a job supporting the sales of IBM computers in a market where the different metrics from all three worlds had to be related. It became my job to figure out the relationships and provide clients with a rational way to choose hardware for their work. There were some forays into availability, solution architecture, and more general "fit for purpose" decision support, but I spent the last 18 years of my time at IBM immersed in the world of comparing architectures, workloads, and performance measurements.

When I came to teach at CCU in 2017, I noticed that there was no course offering in Computer or IT systems performance. Since then, I have taught Architecture, Infrastructure, and introductory IT and Computer Science classes. I was able to offer some insight into performance to my students. This was done on an ad hoc basis with one lecture or module of performance work added to the syllabus.

There is very little course content available that is appropriate for undergraduate introductory classes and also rigorous enough to build a foundation for further study. The material I explored is either too narrow in point of view or more appropriate for advanced study. There are some introductions to queueing theory and systems performance, but they are generally more appropriate for IT practitioners with a specific task or aimed at graduate-level courses in systems and manufacturing engineering.

I found myself creating material for my introductory classes as well as assembling my previously published work. The result is this manuscript, which is a combination of years of professional material and new material that explains IT Performance. The material is suitable for teaching performance in introductory computer sciences and information technology classes. It includes sufficient theory to build foundational intuition and knowledge. It also exposes the reader to some math. We require a significant study of mathematics in our curricula. In my opinion, we don't use enough math in our introductory classes to motivate that study. The math does not have to be laborious, particularly if we present meaningful results and show practical methods using existing analysis tools like spreadsheet software and the R studio. Performance is a very good topic for getting students comfortable with at least some of the math of Computer Sciences. It is also a good framework for the introduction of IT infrastructure and architecture.

ACKNOWLEDGMENTS

I would like to acknowledge first and foremost my wife, Rae Temple, without whom I probably would not have survived to learn what is in this book, let alone to write it. I love you, Rae, much more than you know. I should acknowledge Beth French and Shannon Giagios, and their families, for putting up with the times when I was engaged with this effort instead of them. I also should acknowledge my dad, who introduced me to computers 60 years ago.

Many former IBM colleagues had a large hand in my ability to write this. The IBM Processor Systems engineering teams, the IBM Poughkeepsie Design Center Team, the IBM System Architects Team, the Fit for Purpose "Usual Suspects" Core Team, the IBM Competitive Project Office, and the IBM Systems Group Lab Services Team all made contributions.

Some key individuals from those teams who were particularly influential are Erich Amrehn, Bob Angel, John Banchy, Monte Bauman, Rick Lebsack, Scott Lundell, Gord Palin, Roger Rogers, Bob St. John, John Thomas, Wakaki Thompson, and Daryl Van Nort.

I would like to acknowledge the IBM global technical sales support team and their clients for supplying data, challenging us with issues, and keeping us honest. I would like to thank Len Santalucia, Yongook Kim, and Marty Deitch of Vicom Infinity for supplying an essential set of server utilization data and collaboration with my independent efforts in Performance Architecture.

I would also like to acknowledge the managers and executives who oversaw and supported my later work at IBM. Each of these people had a lasting impact on me personally and professionally. They are diversified in background, age, management style, and point of view. Though my leadership journey started long before I met any of them, they all helped me along the way. I appreciate the time I spent with all of them. Some are still at IBM and others have moved on. They are Mark Anzani, Vinnie Cozzolino, Karl Freund, Paul Fried, Rick Fuchs, Bob Hoey, Kris Jayram, Jeff Nyhart, Dave Latvis, Greg Lotko, George Peterman, Jim Stallings, and Terri Virnig.

Much of the work that is behind this was aided and abetted by the IBM Distinguished Engineer and IBM Fellow community, which was supported and led by IBM Senior VP (retired) Nick Donofrio. In particular, I should acknowledge Guru Rao, my mentor for many years; Don Grice, who helped me understand Supercomputing; and Gary King, who helped me understand mainframe performance. I also acknowledge my cofounders of the IBM Poughkeepsie Design Center, Frank DeGilio, Hilon Potter, and Mike Bliss. I want to thank Rick Lebsack for introducing me to Computer Measurement Group (CMG) and for agreeing to review the draft. I also want to thank my daughter, Beth French, for the Christmas gift of Dr. Hamming's book, which I have used as a reference.

TeamQuest, Inc. deserves acknowledgment for the notion of a "usage-based performance index (UPI)." TeamQuest has used an index that they call "TeamQuest Performance Indicator" (TPI = 100 X Service Time/Response Time). I had been using a wait time/response time to understand relative performance. Both metrics indicate response time without the need to determine Service Time, which is hard to obtain. However, the TPI works better as a figure of merit because it grows with better performance. The math is also simpler for TPI. I dropped the x 100 and changed the name to Usage-based Performance Index (UPI). The math is the same but the TPI is measured using rather sophisticated performance models and measurements. The UPI is a generic metric that does not have the benefit of TeamQuest's portfolio of tools and methods. I developed the UPI v Utilization plot and associated analysis and shared it with TeamQuest folks at a CMG conference, but I don't know if they use it. The plot is a "performance architecture" tool/method, and TeamQuest does monitoring and managing of implemented IT solutions.

REFERENCES

These books have been influential in my understanding of Infrastructure Architecture and Performance and sources of inspiration. This book references them. Much of my professional work of the last two decades stands upon the work of these authors.

In Search of Clusters – The Ongoing Battle in Lowly Parallel Computing, Dr. Gregory Pfister (Pfister)

Guerilla Capacity Planning, Dr. Neil Gunther (Gunther)

Practical Scaling Analysis with the Universal Scaling Law Baron Schwartz (Schwartz)

Infrastructure Architecture – Infrastructure Building Blocks and Concepts Sjaak Laan (Laan)

The Art of Doing Science and Engineering – Learning to Learn, Dr. Richard W. Hamming (Hamm)

Factory Physics – Foundations of Manufacturing Management, Wallace J. Hopp and Mark L. Spearman (Hopp)

Queueing Systems – Volume 2: Computing Applications, Leonard Kleinrock (Klein)

They are all good references. *In Search of Clusters* is also an entertaining read. *...Learning to Learn* gets deep into math but has a lot of insight about doing technical work as a career. It is also a source of quotable material and history about the many aspects of IT to which Dr. Hamming contributed.

Much of the mathematics in this book can be found in *Factory Physics* as a set of "laws" governing the performance of manufacturing systems. When they appear in this book, they will be named and numbered as in *Factory Physics* and will be paraphrased to match a nomenclature appropriate to Information Technology. However, because of the organization of the narrative in this book, they occur in a different order.

I previously published ideas and methods that are discussed in this book.

IBM SYSTEMS MAGAZINE MAINFRAME EDITION:

"Understanding Relative Capacity," March 2003

"A More Effective Comparison Starts with Relative Capacity," July 2012

"Running Highly Stacked Workloads on System z can Greatly Reduce Cost per Unit of Work," March 2013

"Alternative Metrics Deliver a More Complete View of Hardware Performance for Server RFPS," November 2013

PRESENTATIONS/PAPERS AT CMG CONFERENCES

"Relative Capacity and Fit for Purpose Platform Choice," with Roger Rogers, *CMG Journal,* Issue 123, Spring 2009

"Alternative Performance Metrics for Server RFPs," CMG 2013

"Applying Benchmark Data to a Relative Capacity Model," with John Thomas, CMG 2013

"Heisenberg and Utilization," CMG 2014

"A Utilization Study," CMG 2015

"Alternative Performance Metrics for Server RFPs," CMG 2017

"Metrics and Methods to Avoid the ITR Trap," CMG 2017

PUBLISHED ON LINKEDIN.COM

"You Should Seriously Consider LinuxOne," 10/12/2015

"We Don't Understand Utilization," 5/19/2015

"A Fundamental Misunderstanding," 1/9/2015

"More on Metrics," 8/7/2014

"Positioning of 2014 Servers," 6/17/2014

"Common Metrics Don't Work," 6/14/2014

PUBLISHED ON SEEKING ALPHA

"Understand Tech Fundamentals Before Accepting Analyst Assertions About Tech Stocks," Seekingalpha.com, Jan. 23, 2014, 1:44 PM ET

ABOUT THIS BOOK

Performance determines whether or not an IT solution "delivers the goods." This book will lay out the fundamentals of performance, and then take some deep dives into the effect of utilization, performance estimators, and scaling. It develops quantitative and qualitative methods of comparing solution infrastructures' performance.

Important ideas and equations are highlighted in bold text. Whenever I paraphrase a "Law" of *Factory Physics*, the law is stated in the form "Law number: Law name, followed by a statement of the Law." A summary of the IT version of the laws in numerical order is in Appendix B. The original form, related to factory operation, appears in numerical order on pages 622 and 623 of *Factory Physics*.

This book provides an explanation of Dr. Gunther's Universal Scaling Law (USL) found in his book, *Guerrilla Capacity Planning*. A set of scaling models is built by choosing values of the USL parameters. The USL is fundamental to understanding scaling. However, Dr. Gunther's work is ITR centric. Central ideas of this book are that ITR = Threads x Thread Speed and the need to view performance through the eyes of the user and owner as well as the vendor point of view. Dr. Gunther's exposition of the USL does not explicitly show how the USL relates throughput to thread speed or response time. Neither does he relate scaling to saturation. I have renamed some of the elements of the USL to make these relationships more apparent and spend some time on the duality of saturation and scaling. I also modified Gunther's method for regression of scaling data to simplify the process. I have reused examples from both Gunther's and Baron Schwarz's work on the USL, in some cases expanding on them. I added a mainframe scaling example to show how "negative" kappa occurs in scaling data.

Anecdotes written in the first person may occasionally appear in this book. These are not written out of ego but are included to give perspective and offer insight. The concluding material on performance architecture is an update of the tools and methods that I developed and used both at IBM and as an independent consultant. I am republishing them here because the methods are useful and are not to my knowledge gathered together anywhere else.

There are 13 sections in the book. This roughly corresponds to the weeks of a semester, leaving some room for testing review and projects. However, fitting a performance course into an existing curriculum can be an impractical goal, so the book can be used for performance modules in other classes. I hope that university professors find this book a useful source for performance material.

IT professionals and trainers will also find the text useful. Indeed, much of the content of this book was developed in a professional support and training environment

Signal Analysis of Time Series (Capacity Planning), Feed Back (Workload Management and Scheduling), and Queueing Theory (beyond the open queue wait time model) are not covered in this version of the book. The math involved is too advanced for the target of apprentice and undergraduate level students in introductory IT courses.

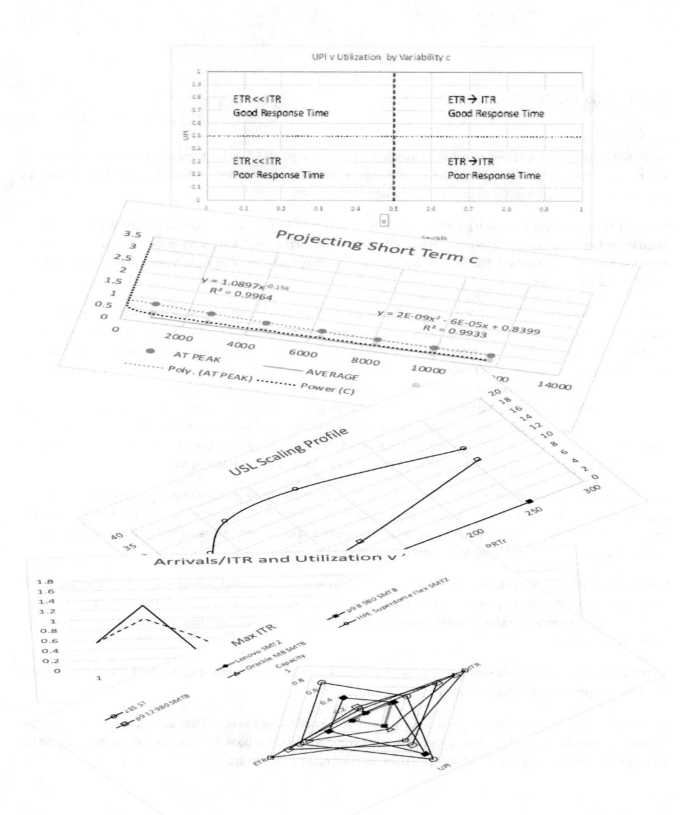

TABLE OF CONTENTS

PART 0: BEFORE DIVING IN

Before we start we need to define a few terms and explain how to get the most out of this book. We will start with some definitions.

Definition 1: Information Technology – the hardware, software, methods, and processes by which information is created, transformed, stored, and shared.

Definition 2: Digital technology – information technology in which information and data are represented by strings of binary bits. Each bit can be either 1 or 0. A bit can be moved, stored, or flipped. The strings represent any message, image, numbers, or commands (instructions).

Definition 3: A computer is a manipulator of digital strings. The main elements are processing cores, memories, input/output (I/O) connections, and a "nest" that ties it all together. Both cores and the nest contain cache memories and buffer storage elements to match the slower speed of the memories and I/O with the higher speed of the cores.

Definition 4: Software provides the instructions that drive the cores. The software will depend on some external process controlled by users. The process and the software implementation can cause an IT solution to be faster or slower and other implementations by changing the "pathlength" required to do the solution's "unit of work."

If you understand the above at a high level, you should be able to understand the nomenclature in this book.

To get the most out of this book, you should pay attention to the following.

1. There is a lot of math in here. I have worked to avoid advanced mathematics. High school algebra will work for you in most instances. However, the "math centric" material is typically contained in text boxes so that you can decide to skip, gloss over, or work to understand them depending on your needs and desires.
2. Important equations and ideas are printed in bold italics and isolated sentences between paragraphs.
3. The "laws" of *Factory Physics* hold for the analysis of the performance of any system. Here they are applied to Information Technology. The main difference between IT and industrial applications is the magnitude of time and speed. IT work varies from very small (flip one bit) to very large (model the weather), but it is made up of billions of tiny work units. Time is very short (sub-nanosecond) but can run continuously for years. Also, in industrial applications materials are conserved, but in IT data is malleable.
4. The book is composed of interrelated parts. It is fruitful to watch for the interconnections.

This book is for anyone who works on, studies, or seriously uses Information Technology. Students will gain important insights into how the technology works. Practitioners will find a fresh perspective. The material spans from fundamentals to the results of new research. This book will provide a background for those new to the subject and fresh insights for professional practitioners.

PART 1: PERFORMANCE FUNDAMENTALS

I once was a host at our development lab's open house. We were demonstrating the prototype of our new computer. Someone asked, "What does it do?" I had to think about the answer. In those days most people did not interact directly with computers. They interacted with people or institutions that used computers. They might fill out forms or answer surveys, from which data entry was done. Their credit card bill or hours worked record might be in the form of a punched card. This was as close as they would likely get to a computer other than watching flashing lights or spinning tape drives on a movie or TV show. The machine I was showing them had no flashing lights and there were no tape drives attached. I was forced to say: "It just sits there, makes noise with the fans, and heats the room." Physically, this is about all we can say about any IT equipment. Mechanically they are heaters that are sometimes noisy.

Performance is the only way to answer the question "What does a computer do?" If there is no performance, computers are noisy heaters.

We relate performance to speed. We think of speed in terms of mechanics. A vehicle travels from point A to point B. We measure how long it takes. Something moves; it takes time to make the move. By measuring the time, we can measure the speed or rate at which the movement takes place. Note that this is an average. During the journey, a vehicle may encounter traffic controls, heavy traffic, and various terrain and road conditions. The speed will vary at various points along the way.

Performance is also associated with the rate at which work is done. A pump fills jugs. It takes an hour to fill 50 5-gallon jugs. The pump's performance is 5 X 50 = 250 gallons per hour. You go to get a 5-gallon jug. How long does it take? Do you experience a pump filling 50 jugs per hour? Suppose most of the jugs are 50 gallons, but some are 100 gallons. Suppose when you arrive, there are already people waiting for jugs. Now how long does it take to get your jug? Is your journey to and from the pump part of the time it takes to get your jug?

Does the pump's performance change if it takes you a minute or an hour to get your jug? Suppose the pump's source periodically gets cut off because the reservoir needs to be refilled. How does this affect the performance of the pump? How does this affect the time it takes for you to get your jug? Now suppose that the liquid being pumped is altered along the way. Some jugs are filled with "Red," others "Blue," and some "Purple." Suppose Purple is made by repumping Blue liquid through the add-Red process. Purple takes longer to make than Red or Blue. Does the pump's performance change? How does the demand for Purple affect how long you wait for your jug of Blue? What if you are waiting for Red?

You can think of an IT solution as a pump. It is not pumping a physical liquid; it is pumping information. IT performance is about the rate at which information is moved from place to place while being transformed during certain parts of the journey. In the end, we measure IT performance as a rate at which the information of interest flows.

Anyone watching a computer without access to the resulting information will see a box that does nothing.

THROUGHPUT

The flow of work in any system is known as throughput. The throughput of a factory is measured in units produced divided by the time to produce them. Units/Hour, Units/Day, or Units/Week will be used depending on how long it takes an individual unit to be produced. The time to produce a toothpick will be less than the time to produce an integrated circuit or an automobile. The throughput of a transportation system is passenger miles/time.

LAW 1: Little's Law Throughput = Work Done / Time.

For information systems, the throughput of a solution, system, or computer varies depending on the work. Since computers are governed by clock cycles, the most primitive measurement of throughput is the clock rate, which is measured in cycles per second or Hertz (Hz). The clock rate is a *simple and useful proxy for the speed of information flow.*

Computing cores process information by executing sequences of instructions fetched from memory. The number of cycles per instruction is dependent on the Instruction Set Architecture (ISA), the organization of the processor hardware, and the mix of instructions included in the "instruction stream" doing the work. This leads to the first refinement of clock rate as the proxy for speed. This metric is "Instructions per Second."

IPS = (Instructions/cycle) (cycles/second)

There are many possible instruction streams to choose from to create this metric. Depending on the workload, various instruction streams are measured to create more realistic measures of information flow such as queries/time, transactions/time, job steps/time, or dialog steps/time.

Performance must be considered from three perspectives:

1. The Vendors'

2. The Owners'

3. The Users'

Performance is in the eye of the beholder

THE VENDOR

Almost all performance metrics commonly associated with IT performance are based on the vendor perspective. Some of these are:

- MHz – Clock cycles per second

- MIPS – Million instructions per second

- FLOPS – Floating point operations per second

- TPMC – Transactions per minute on transaction processing council benchmark "C"

- TPCH – Queries per minute on transaction processing council benchmark "H"

- SAPs – Dialog steps per minute on the SAP SD module benchmark

- SPECint – Performance of a group of programs doing Integer Arithmetic

- SPECjbb – Performance of a group of programs running Java

- SPECjapp – Performance of a group of programs running Java applications

- SPECfp – Performance of a group of programs running Floating-Point Arithmetic

All of these metrics are called Intrinsic (aka Internal) Throughput Rate (ITR) metrics. They measure the sustained rate at which information is processed when the system is running at or near 100% utilization. For our pump example, 250 Gallons per Hour is an ITR metric. There are multiple metrics listed above because there are many different types of workloads. Each machine does not do all workloads as well as others.

Each vendor will market their equipment based on the workloads that run the best for them. They will never agree on a single metric because they compete for business based on their performance. Vendors will only support and publish metrics that show their equipment as superior or competitive.

Today's computers often consist of multiple processing cores. The most primitive ITR metric for modern multi-core system systems is known as "MHz" (megahertz) to Intel users.

ITR ~ Clock Speed x Cores

Many modern processors can run multiple instruction streams per processor core. The resources in the operating system and the hardware that enables this are called threads. A particular solution implementation may be limited by the application software's ability to use all the provided hardware threads. It can also be limited by the operating system's or hardware's ability to make threads available.

A generally applicable definition of ITR is Thread Speed x Thread Count:

ITR = S_t x Threads

Little's Law for computers: ITR is ALWAYS Thread Speed x Threads (The Vendors' Law)

This equation holds regardless of workload, instruction stream of interest, hardware design, or Instruction Set Architecture. The main objective of performance measurement to determine thread speed, as the thread count of any combination of hardware and software is always a given. To determine performance, we need to determine the speed at which they run.

Estimating thread speed for multithreaded cores

Some vendors provide simultaneous multithreading (SMT) to improve ITR. We need a way to estimate ITR when multiple threads are operating simultaneously on each core. The improvement provided is significantly less than the number of additional threads provided. Estimates vary with workload and machine design. We refine the Clock x Cores estimate of ITR for multithreaded machines by using the ratio of Estimated Improvement / Threads per Core:

S_t ~Clock Rate x Improvement/Threads per Core

This gives us the refined estimator for multithreaded cores:

ITR ~ Clock Rate x Cores x Improvement

The maximum reported improvement for 2, 4, and 8 threads per core are on the order of:

ITR(2) <= 1.7 ITR(1) → S_t (2) ~ .855 S_t (1)

ITR(4) <= 1.35 ITR(1) → S_t (4) ~ .5255 S_t (1)

ITR(8) <= 2.96 ITR(1) → S_t (8) ~ .375 S_t (1)

These are for the IBM Power 9 processor. IBM's z14 and z15 and Intel's Xeon processors report ITR(2) ~ 1.3 ITR(1), (St~0.65) and they do not implement ITR(4) or ITR(8).

Any further refinement of ITR metrics requires the measurement of thread speed while running a specific type of work over a sustained period. The main goal of most performance measurements is to establish a thread speed to apply to the ITR equation. The actual behavior of a set of processing cores running SMT depends on the ability of software to use all the cores and the cache miss ratio that results from running the software at hand. The vendor SMT improvement metrics are measured using optimized software, with near-optimal cache miss rates[1]. If the cache miss rate is too low, the threads contend for processor resources more than the measured load. If the cache miss rate is too high, the threads contend for cache and memory more than the measured load. The following chart illustrates the situation.

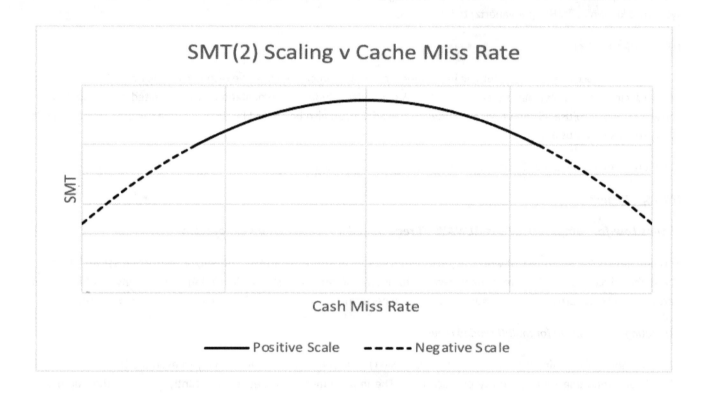

---

[1] The cache miss rate is the rate at which data required by the processor is not found in a cache, causing a delay while it is fetched from slower, larger storage. Thread speed is inversely related to cache miss rate.

THE OWNER

The owner of an IT solution needs to understand its value. Owner metrics need to reflect what happens when the business process and users drive the machine, rather than the rated throughput potential of the machine. The owner wants to have a $/day value metric for the work performed by the solution. This is obtained by discounting the ITR, taking into account the utilization of the hardware.

If the business process and users do not exploit the full potential of the machine, utilization can be significantly lower than 100%. Many processes and user-driven loads vary significantly with time. The total work done per day is less than the ITR would indicate. Some loads have a dependency on data residing on storage devices or network connections. If the processing elements have sufficient ITR, they can outrun the arrival of data and go into I/O wait states. This reduces the utilization.

We name the owner view metrics Effective (aka External) Throughput Rate (ETR). We define it as a function of ITR and utilization.

$ETR(t) = ITR\ f(u(t))$

We estimate ETR as:

$ETR(t) \sim ITR(t)\ u(t)$

$ETR_{avg} \sim ITR\ u_{avg}$

Law 5: ETRavg < ITR (The Owners' Law)

THE USER

The user of an IT solution rarely experiences either ITR or ETR. In most cases, they experience response time. In our pump example, Response Time (Tr) is the time it takes you to get your jug filled. This will change depending on how many other people have arrived to fill a jug just before you got there. Response Time is defined as the sum of Service Time (Ts) and Wait Time (Tw).

LAW 13: Response Time = Service Time + Wait Time (The Users' Law)

T_r is inversely related to Thread speed and ITR. It is also governed by the parallelism or lack thereof in the work done to create a response for the user. We can bound T_r.

$$\frac{1}{ITR} \leq T_r \leq \frac{1}{S_T}$$

There is a whole subject in system science known as queueing theory. It describes the rather complex relationship between Wait Time (Tw) and Arrival rates, utilization, Service rates, and ITR. According to the theory:

$$T_w = f(T_s, u, c)$$

where u is utilization and c is the variability of the load.

In general, Tw increases with Ts, utilization, and load variability. The simplest queuing model that takes all three of these factors into account is:

$$T_r \sim T_s \left(1 + \frac{c^2 u}{1-u}\right)$$

Note that this is expressed as an estimator since the applicable queueing model is often more complex.

T_s is difficult to obtain. We define a Usage-Based Performance Indicator $UPI = \frac{T_s}{T_r}$

This gives us:
$$UPI \sim \frac{1}{\left(1 + \frac{c2u}{1-u}\right)}$$

Tr becomes unbounded at u=1, **UPI** → 0 as **u** → 1.

LAW 8: (Utilization) Tr has an unbounded nonlinear relationship to utilization and ETR.

Initial Summary of Performance Estimators

The Vendor View

ITR = Threads x Thread Speed

ITR ~ Cores x Clk Rate

ITR ~ Cores x Clk Rate x Threading Improvement

The Owner View

ETR = ITR x f(u)

ETR(u) ~ ITR x u

ETR ~ ITR x Uavg

The User View

$T_r \sim T_s \times (1 + c^2 u/(1-u))$

$UPI = 1/(1 + c^2 u/(1-u))$

PART 2: THE FUNDAMENTAL TRADE-OFF OF IT PERFORMANCE

From the owners' point of view, the business value is directly related to ETR. For the users, value is inversely related to Tr. Both ETR and Tr increase with utilization. For now, we will make the simplifying assumption:

ETR(u) ~ ITR x u

If this model holds, utilization is a good proxy for ETR. Owners will drive average utilization as high as possible, deriving maximum value from their IT investment. Because T_r also increases with utilization, this practice detracts from the user experience by making the solution slower. This is a tradeoff. We cannot maximize ETR while minimizing Tr.

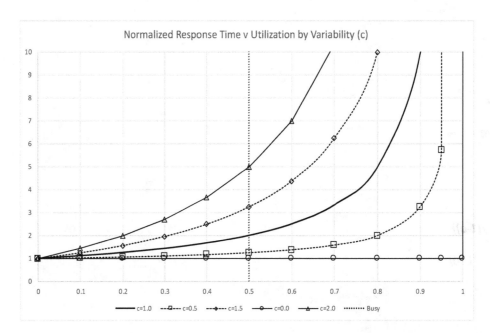

This is a generalized form of the illustration of the tradeoff between Tr and ETR, known as the "Response Time v Utilization" plot. The dashed line is the "Busy" line at 50% utilization. Any solution running a less than 50% utilization is waiting for work or data most of the time. The bold black line, where c = 1 represents "moderate" variability, also represents an elementary queueing model in which variability is assumed to be moderate.

Most ITR measurements are done with loads that have variability considerably less than 1 or tolerate response times which are considerably greater than double the service time, or both. Most interactive applications and transaction workloads have relatively high variability and more stringent response time requirements. Since it is difficult to determine T_s and because we want a positive performance metric for the user view, we defined UPI = T_s/T_r. This inverts the response time metric into a positive performance or "speed" metric. It effectively normalizes the result to $T_s = 1$ as in the chart above. Here is the framework for understanding the UPI v u plot:

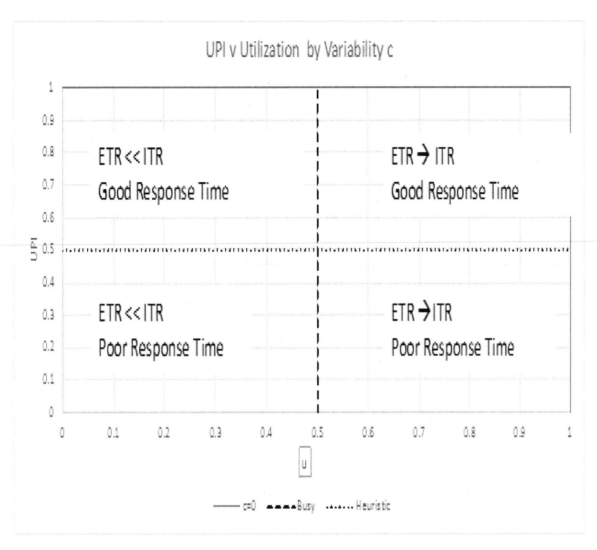

UPI v Utilization by Variability c

ETR << ITR
Good Response Time

ETR → ITR
Good Response Time

ETR << ITR
Poor Response Time

ETR → ITR
Poor Response Time

UPI

u

——— c=0   ▪▪▪▪ Busy   ······· Heuristic

We drew a heuristic line across the chart at UPI = 0.5. UPI above the line is better than UPI below the line. The Busy Line remains at 50% utilization. ETR approaches ITR to the right of this line. These lines break the chart into four quadrants. It is desirable to operate the solution in the upper-right quadrant.

When we put data onto the chart, it becomes apparent that we cannot get into the upper-right quadrant unless the variability is low (c < 1). It is also clear that high variability leads to operation at low utilization or to undesirable response time.

LAW 6: (Variability) ETR can only approach ITR at good Tr if variability is low.

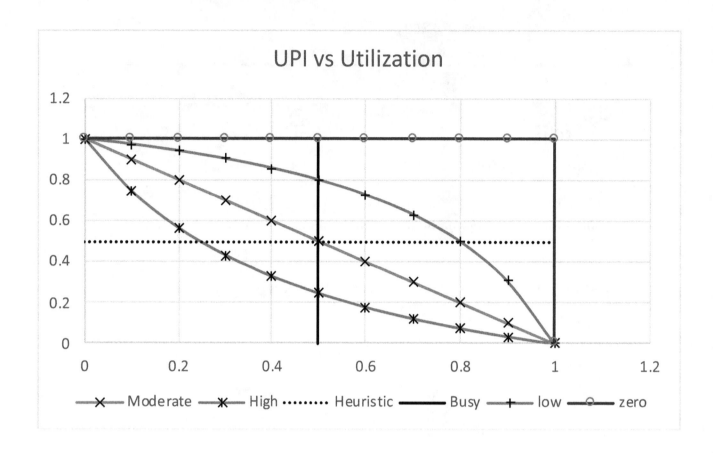

UPI vs Utilization

UPI allows us to understand response time behavior without knowing the service time.

PART 3: UTILIZATION

External Throughput Rate (ETR) and Response Time (T_r) were shown to be functions of "Utilization." The simplest definition of Utilization is "the fraction of time during which the hardware is busy." In an IT system time is quantized into discrete cycles. Utilization becomes:

Utilization = Busy Cycles/Elapsed Cycles

The fundamental unit of capacity in a computer is the core. At any cycle, cores are either busy or idle. Because of the binary nature of core utilization at any instance (cycle), each core utilization is either 1 or it is 0. For short intervals, peak utilization of a core is always 1. Core utilization values that are not 1 or 0 only emerge after multiple cycles elapse. After an interval of i cycles, the average utilization of a core can be in i + 1 states. They are represented by the series of core utilization states $0, 1/t, 2/t, 3/t...(i-1)/t, 1$.

The measured utilization is an average that emerges by counting busy cores and cycles. The server utilization at any cycle is:

Utilization = Busy Cores/(Configured Cores)

In computers, both time and capacity are "quantized." Since utilization is measured by counting busy cores and cycles, utilization is quantized as well. It is *always* measured as an average over a time interval, which makes utilization a statistic.

If the load is variable over time, there will be an associated deviation from the long interval average utilization (Uavg) for each interval of time. The deviation from the Uavg diminishes as the size of the interval over which utilization is measured gets longer. As the interval increases, the values smooth out and approach the long interval average utilization. As the interval decreases, the values diverge toward the quantized idle and busy states.

For a system containing one single-threaded processor core, it is only through averaging over some discrete time intervals (cycles) that utilization values between 0 and 1 emerge. In the very short run, time becomes quantized into cycles. These first appear as system (dispatch) cycles on the order of milliseconds. At extremely short intervals, time is quantized into machine (clock) cycles.

In the short run, the peak utilization of a uniprocessor is always 1 (100% busy). As we introduce more cores, capacity also appears in discrete quanta. At any instance in time, each core is either busy or it is not. As the number of cores increases, the relative size of the quanta shrinks. The instantaneous utilization will always be busy cores/total cores. Since we cannot create fractional processors, this is a ratio of positive integers. The number of instantaneous utilization states that the machine can take is 1+ p, where p is the number of cores.

If there are more cores available than the software can activate in the short run, the peak utilization will be less than 1. It will be impossible to achieve the states with busy threads beyond the state at which all software threads are running concurrently. However, for many loads, there are busy periods with more potentially active software threads than the hardware can activate concurrently. In the short run, the measurable peak approaches 1 even for multiple multithreaded cores.

At 100%, we say that work becomes "stacked" on the threads of the machine. This means that there is active work waiting in queues. As we shorten the interval, it becomes more likely that during some intervals, enough threads are active for queues to form. When this happens, work becomes "stacked."

Processor affinity is the practice of pinning pieces of work to specific cores and perhaps pinning data to real memory near them. In that case, some cores can have stacked work, while some are busy with one thread, and others are idle. The maximum potential peak utilization of the machine is 100% unless there is a software or workload limit to the concurrent thread count lower than the number of available threads in the machine.

ILLUSTRATION: THE QUANTIZATION OF CAPACITY AND UTILIZATION
Given p available cores, the utilization state and quanta are given by

States(p) = p + 1

Quantum(p) = 1/p

At ten available cores, each busy core/cycle causes a 10% leap in utilization. At two available cores, the leap is 50%.

Processors	Utilization States	Quantum	Fraction
1	2	1.0000	1/1
2	3	0.5000	1/2
3	4	0.3333	1/3
4	5	0.2500	1/4
5	6	0.2000	1/5
6	7	0.1667	1/6
7	8	0.1429	1/7
8	9	0.1250	1/8
9	10	0.1111	1/9
10	11	0.1000	1/10
16	17	0.0625	1/16
32	33	0.0313	1/32
64	65	0.0156	1/64
100	101	0.0100	1/100
128	129	0.0078	1/128

You need 100 cores for the utilization quanta to drop to 1%. As cycles accumulate, the measured utilization will take on values made by averaging discrete values represented by an integer number of quanta. For a system with four cores, the measured utilization will be built by averaging the values (0, 0.25, 0.50, 0.75, 1.00) on a cycle-by-cycle basis. Any measured value that occurs between these five values is a function of the averaging and never actually occurs at any cycle. In all modern computers, both computing resources and time are quantized. Time is quantized in clock cycles, and resources are quantized in "cores."

Time increments in cycles. Processing is added by cores. At each cycle, each core is either busy or idle.

Utilization is measured by counting Busy Cores/Configured Core each cycle for n cycles. The utilization for the interval is the average of this count over the many cycles that make up the measurement interval,

u_n = *Sum(Busy Cores$_i$/Configured Cores$_i$)/n*.

where n is the count of cycles per interval.

As measured, utilization is always an average over n cycles per interval.

When n increases, the range of values of u(t) converges toward the overall average (Uavg). When n decreases, the range of values for each core expands away from the average toward 1 and 0. As a result, the measured variability of the workload increases as the interval n decreases. Since each core's utilization spreads toward the extremes, the overall machine utilization does as well.

The extent to which this occurs depends on how the business process drives work on the cores. If the peaks of core utilizations are correlated, then the spread in machine utilization of the machine is maximized. If not, the machine peaks remain somewhere between the average and the extremes. Very often there is some interval size that is short enough for peaks at 100% utilization to appear. Response time will suffer during these peaks if they are sufficiently long enough to grow long queues of stacked work. For the same interval size, one or more troughs will reach a minimum that approaches zero.

Utilization as a Random Variable

Utilization is measured as an average and is typically driven by a randomly varying load. The combination makes utilization a statistic. To understand how it affects performance, we must understand the fundamentals of statistics.

If the business process varies randomly, then utilization is also a random variable. This means that there is uncertainty in how it varies over time. Random variables need to be described by a pair of numbers rather than a single value. Conventionally, we represent them by the expected value or mean and a standard deviation. Mean and expected value are alternative terms for "average," which represents the center of the distribution of values.

The mean is calculated as the sum of the values divided by the number of values:

m = Sum(x$_i$)/n

The Standard Deviation is calculated as the square root of the sum of the squared deviations from the mean divided by n-1:

s = (Sum(x$_i$ – m)^2/(n-1))$^{1/2}$

For large n, the standard deviation approaches the square root of the average of the squared deviations from the mean in the sample. Fortunately, we do not have to calculate this by hand. Average and standard deviation functions are readily available in spreadsheet applications like Excel, statistical program packages like R, and programming languages like Python, Java, and C.

SPECIFYING RANDOM VALUES

The value of a Random Variable X is given by:

$$X = m + ks$$

The probability of X having any particular value depends on the distribution. Generally, small absolute values of k are more likely than large absolute values of k.

Assuming that the load "just fits" into the system, the value of the random variable for utilization u(n) is:

$$u(n) = X_n / X_{max}$$

It is very common to design solutions such that the denominator is larger than sampled Xmax, leaving room for growth and variation beyond the sampled values. If the system cannot contain Xmax, then u(n) will reach 1 at $X_n < X_{max}$. The system will saturate, spending too much time at 100% utilization with poor performance. For $X_{100} < X_{max}$:

$$U(n) = min(1, X_n / X_{100})$$

ROGERS' EQUATION (AND DEFINITION OF THE COEFFICIENT OF VARIABILITY C)

There is an equation for average utilization derived by Roger Rogers at IBM.[2] We will assume here that the demand for services on the solution is a random variable with mean m and a standard deviation s.

Utilization = the mean demand m divided by the capacity:

$u_{avg} = m/(1+ k_{max}s)$

The parameter kmax is the number of standard deviations from the mean that the load has to reach to drive the system to its maximum utilization.

Multiplying by m/m yields this equation:

$u_{avg} = 1/(1+ k_{max}s/m)$

s/m is the definition of the statistic "Index of Variability," c. This is the same c that we took for granted earlier. Given that, we have:

$u_{avg} = 1/(1+ k_{max}c)$

This is Rogers' equation for a single load on a single server. The use of c is a standard statistical method for quantifying variability. A more intuitive measure of variability is the ratio of the peak to the average. Notice that for most systems the instantaneous peak of any load is at 100% utilization or u(t)=1. We rearrange the equation as:

$1/u_{avg} = (1+ k_{max}c)$

This form relates the statistic c to the intuitive peak to average ratio

$P/A = u_{max}(1+ k_{max}c)$

If $u_{max} = 1$ $P/A = (1+ k_{max}c)$

---

[2] This is derived in "Relative Capacity and Fit for Purpose Platform Choice," with Roger Rogers, *CMG Journal* Issue 123, Spring 2009. I sometimes call it Roger's equation because he is my friend and coauthor.

UTILIZATION STATISTICS

Most introductions to probability and statistics spend a great deal of time on the "normal" distribution. The normal distribution has the following characteristics:

1. The mean (average) is at the center of the data. To illustrate, we need to define the median and the mode. The median of a distribution is the value that is equal to or less than half the values and larger than or equal to the other half. The mode is the value that occurs more often than any other value. In a normal distribution, the mean, median, and mode all have the same value.

2. All normal distributions have symmetric tails to the left and right of the center.

3. For all normal distributions (where k is in standard deviations):

   - ~5/100 of the distribution occurs above k = 2

   - ~3/1000 of the distribution occurs above k = 3

   - ~3/1,000,000 of the distribution occurs above k = 6

If you examine sample data for utilization, you will not find a normal distribution. There are several reasons for this.

1. Utilization is bounded between 0 and 1.

2. Quantization of short-term data spreads values toward the extremes.

3. If the average is above or below 0.5, the spread is asymmetrical.

Because of this utilization, distributions often have long and/or fat "tails." As the ETR approaches the ITR, the operation enters into the upper tail of the distribution. We have to be more conservative about results than we would if we assumed "normal" statistics. In practice, this means that we must configure systems for higher values of k than in "normal" situations. This tends to reduce utilization along with ETR.

THE BOUNDS OF UTILIZATION (AN ILLUSTRATION)

We always measure an average utilization. Except with the trivial case of constant load, utilization varies as a function of time. The variation is due to a combination of cyclic and random events. Since there are many such events in a workload, we approximate the distribution of load and utilization as a random value. Because of this, we use statistics to describe the utilization. Typically, we calculate the "average utilization" as the mean of measurements taken at intervals over a relatively long period.

For example, we might use one-minute interval data taken over a day. We calculate the standard deviation from the data and then define the peak as the maximum interval value, in terms of several standard deviations from the mean, typically represented by the symbol k_{max}.

Because utilization is bounded to be between 0 and 1, it can have a near normal distribution only if the mean is near enough to 50% and the standard deviation is small. As the mean moves away from 50%, there will be an abundance of zero and/or one value in the distribution, skewing it away from normal by creating a "fat tail."

Conventionally, the upper tail of a distribution starts at k = 3, which for a normal distribution represents the values above the region in which 0.997 of the instances occur. The median is the value in the distribution in which half of the values fall above and half fall below. The mode is the value in the distribution at which the maximum number of samples occurs.

In a normal distribution the mean, the median, and the mode all fall at the same point, which is the average value. When a fat tail occurs, the median and mode shift away from the mean and there are more instances than the normal distribution predicts beyond k = 3. Because of the bounded nature of utilization, increasing the range of the load on the system eventually leads to an increase in the number short term values at the extremes of 0 and 1. This naturally leads to long and fat tails. Adding capacity tends to pile up values on the lower tail, making it fat. Adding load tends to pile up values in the upper tail, making it fat. As a result, utilization distributions are rarely normal and typically have fat tails, unless the variability is very low.

HEADROOM

Relative headroom (HR) is the ratio of the capacity remaining to the capacity used. Mathematically this is written as:

$HR(u) = (1-u)/u$

This is the inverse of the utilization term of the equation for response time. Response time is inversely proportional to relative headroom.

It can be shown from Rogers' equation that

$HR_{avg} = k_{100}c$

TAIL DISTORTION.

Here is an illustration of how tail distortion occurs in utilization distributions. Suppose we have a normally distributed load, with moderate variance. We have a range of machines upon which to place the loads. With the load applied, the average utilization ranges from 0.1 on the largest machine to 0.7 on the smallest. Here are the load distributions scaled to average utilization = average load.

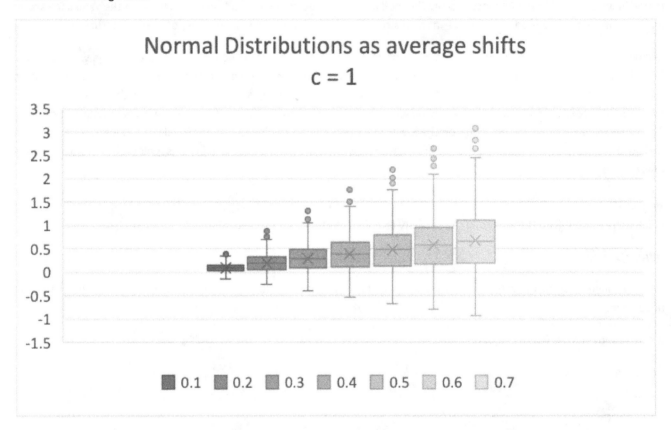

Notice that the load on all the machines spills beyond the bounds of utilization. This is a sample from a normal distribution with the mean shifted and c =1 in all cases. Notice the high-end outlier points (dots). This sample is already skewed a bit. All the machines have instances below zero, and only the smallest have maximums below one. Negative values are not possible. The actual utilization values must value between zero and one. This forces a minimum of zero and a maximum of one.

Here is what happens to the distributions when applied to the machines.

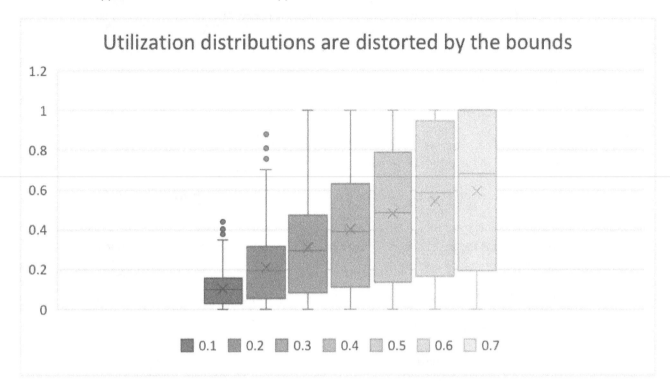

REDUCTION OF VARIABILITY

There are two ways to reduce variability. The first is to modify the process to remove the random variability of the arrival rate. This is known as "batching" the load. Message queues are a type of automated batching, using message queuing software. . Batching can also be accomplished by the process which generates the load.

The second way is sharing system resources among multiple workloads. This is known as consolidation. It is done through multiprogramming and the connection of users, data, and applications to shared resources.

Here is an illustration of how consolidation works. Independent random variables with normal distributions are added in the following manner:

m(X+Y) = m(X) + m(Y)

s(X+Y) = (s(X)² + s(Y)²)¹ᐟ²

Recall that $c = s/m$. Since the SQRT of the sum of the squares is always less than the sum, variability, c, is reduced through consolidation. We can use this to estimate the distribution of combined or consolidated workloads, but we have to understand that this estimator will be optimistic because utilization distributions are rarely totally independent and never normal.

The sum of the averages holds, but the resulting distribution usually has a greater standard deviation than this will calculate. It is always best to use the raw data and do an interval-by-interval summation to determine the resulting distribution. We are left with a situation in which the "statistical sum" will underestimate the peak of the sum, and the sum of the peaks will overestimate it.

SUMMARY

We can now assert the following:

1. Utilization is derived from measurements of quantized time and capacity.

2. Utilization is always measured as an average over an interval.

3. At sufficiently short intervals most systems will peak at 100% and experience lows near 0% utilization.

4. At sufficiently long intervals the range will converge toward the long-term Uavg.

5. Increasing the interval length reduces the measured standard deviation, while the average over a large number of intervals is not affected. This is known as "smoothing."

6. Utilization distributions are not "normal" and often require kmax values greater than the conventional k = 3 designs.

7. Average utilization is a function of $HR_{avg} = k_{max}c$. kmax is a design parameter that determines the service level of the configured system, and c is the statistic for load variability. This is important when dealing with bursty loads and the fat tails associated with utilization distributions.

8. It should be clear that low variability of the load is key to reducing T_r and increasing ETR.

9. Batching and consolidation are two paths to a reduction of variability.

10. The smoothing of measured utilization data tends to reduce the measured variability. This does not affect the overall average, but it does reduce the measured standard deviation.

   Utilization is not a normal statistic.

PART 4: AN EXAMPLE USING REAL SERVER UTILIZATION DATA

Here is a chart of real utilization data from a real IT server. The data is taken every fifteen minutes for roughly five days. There are 475 intervals of utilization data recorded.

We can see that there is a daily cycle of load, but significant random changes between the fifteen-minute intervals. From this data, we create running averages at longer intervals.

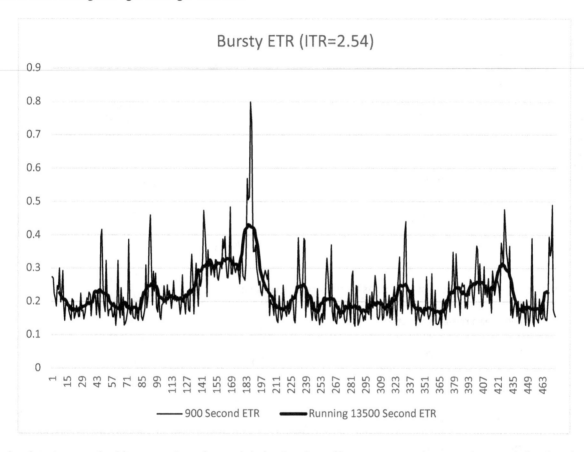

When the data is smoothed by averaging, the peak behavior that affects response time gets lost, and the data becomes dominated by the longer-term cycles. If the data is collected for several weeks, the weekly, monthly, and quarterly cycles will emerge. These are important to the business, particularly in determining business value. However, it is perilous to ignore the peaking behavior of shorter intervals.

Here is another way to look at it:

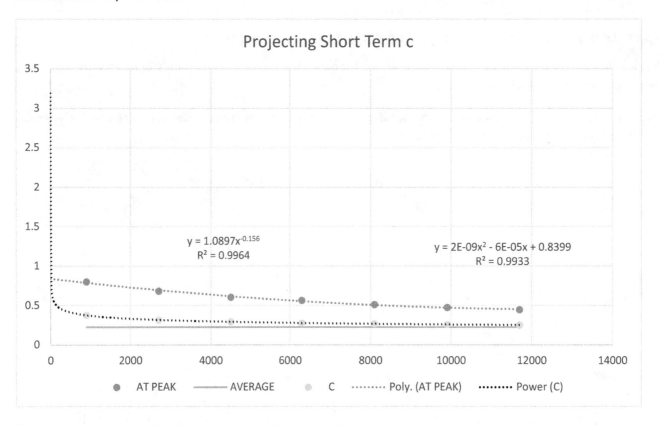

Projecting Short Term c

$y = 1.0897x^{-0.156}$
$R^2 = 0.9964$

$y = 2E\text{-}09x^2 - 6E\text{-}05x + 0.8399$
$R^2 = 0.9933$

● AT PEAK ——— AVERAGE ● C ·········· Poly. (AT PEAK) ········ Power (C)

Here is the resulting behavior of the statistics. As interval size increases:

a. The mean remains constant

b. The maximum decreases

c. The minimum increases

d. The standard deviation decreases

e. The c, kmax, and HR decrease

The use of long interval utilization causes an underestimation of the randomness that drives response time. If the workload is interactive, we are often looking to achieve response times on the order of one second or less. The use of fifteen-minute measurement intervals doesn't work for establishing variability and peak values. However, all is not lost. We can estimate the missing variability data by projecting values from the raw data plus the longer-term running averages of the raw data. This is not rigorous but does allow us to increase the Stdev and c statistics rationally.

The method works this way. We make several sets of long-term data by calculating the running averages of the raw data. We did this to make the charts and tables above. We then express the interval size in seconds (or shorter units of time). We do a regression analysis to create trend equations. We then extrapolate the standard deviation and c statistics to short intervals. This can easily be done with an Excel spreadsheet and scatter graph, but any form of regression analysis works and may be more precise. As the interval size decreases, the variability index moves from low to moderate and then high for very short periods. In this case, the moderate variability is customarily defined as $c=1$. This projection shows that this occurs near one-second intervals.

This method is not theoretically rigorous. There are conditions in the data that can cause it to break down. For example, as the average data approaches zero, c inflates even if the standard deviation is relatively small. Here we resolved this by using the ETR rather than utilization values. The best fit projection is usually either a polynomial or a power curve. It is hard to predict which works better.

SO, WHAT DO WE DO?

In many cases, we have to use the utilization data that is available. It is a long, hard road to justify the processing overhead and data storage to get short interval data. On the other hand, we need to design solutions to avoid poor user experience and we need to understand how growing will affect existing solutions and when performance issues will emerge.

We project that for the measured intervals, this ETR remains less than ITR. At extremely short intervals the projection will break down and the machine will sometimes run at the ITR. We now have to determine acceptable response time. For an interactive load (Case 1) we accept < two-second maximum response time. For a batch load (Case 2) we accept one-minute periods of saturation. We now make a UPI Operating Plot for the two cases plus the raw fifteen-minute interval data.

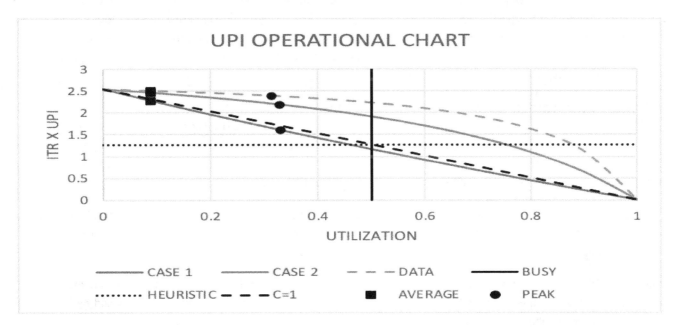

It is clear that to meet the response time requirement for Case 1, we must keep the utilization low because $c > 1$. It is also clear that adding load in Case 2 has less impact on response time than Case 1 because the projected variability is lower. There is more room for Case 2. Both cases run at lower ETR/ITR than would be indicated by the measured data.

PART 5: CONSOLIDATION AND DISTRIBUTION

A BRIEF HISTORY

The most expensive parts of modern IT solutions are the procedures, hardware, and software that allow people and programs to share data at high bandwidth and low latency. Near the beginning of computing, it was all very expensive. As a result, the computer was typically a resource shared by many users for multiple purposes. Naturally, the original operating systems evolved to service a consolidated workload environment. This was how commercial computing came to be dominated by the IBM mainframe. After several generations, IBM eventually developed System 360. Modern mainframes are descended from it; as of this writing, the current instance is known as the IBM z15.

Between the late 1960s and the early 1990s, advances in electronics made it possible to offer lower-cost machines. This was first accomplished with "mini-computer" designs based on integrate circuits. Later on, Very Large Scale Integration (VLSI) processors dominated computer technology. These lower-cost machines could be distributed throughout an enterprise. They were put in factories, warehouses, laboratories, branch offices, retail stores, departmental offices, etc. Along the way, the personal computer and its relatives (Unix workstations, point of sale computers, warehouse workstations) emerged. The network infrastructure to support the online interconnection of personal, departmental, and enterprise machines was established. By the 1990s, this had evolved into the Internet and World Wide Web. Eventually, we began to carry our computers around with us in the form of smartphones and tablets.

It was not lost on the owners of computing systems nor upon vendors that the distributed form of computing hardware was much less expensive to build than mainframes. During the 1980s, distribution of work started to occur in the central data centers as owners sought ways to exploit the lower-cost hardware and bring computing resources closer to workers. At the same time vendors started putting together large aggregations of relatively small computing "nodes" together with high-speed switch hardware to build Massively Parallel Processing (MPP) supercomputers. In the 1990s, IBM started using the microprocessor technology to build mainframes and created Parallel Sysplex, which is a way to exploit parallelism in enterprise computing, through Shared Expanded Storage.

As a result, computer performance came to be thought of as Intrinsic Throughput Rate. The focus was on the rated throughput of the individual nodes and how many nodes could be aggregated. This is how the ITR ~ cores x clock rate metric came to be used. The fundamental idea of distributed processing is that hardware is inexpensive enough that low utilization is not an issue. As long as this is true, distributed processing can work. However, an individual load typically has high headroom requirements that drive the average utilization very low when interactive response times are required.

The outcome of this adventure is known as "server sprawl." While the hardware purchase price remains competitive, the operational cost of dozens, hundreds, or thousands of servers became a large burden to a data center. It became quite common for an enterprise to not even know how many servers they owned.

In the late 1990s, enterprises were running out of space, cooling, and power for their servers. Owners began to look seriously at the consolidation of their server infrastructures. However, Windows, Unix, and Linux environments had been primarily optimized for the distributed computing paradigm.

Something new was needed. IBM enabled Unix and then Linux on the mainframe with its LPAR and VM virtualization to provide a solution. Many clients were becoming committed to Linux on Intel or were locked into Microsoft Windows. Virtualization was reinvented by VMware around 1999, and the idea of consolidation to remove server sprawl began in earnest.

In the 1990s, the parallel supercomputer, mainframe, and distributed server worlds collided. Throughout the current century, there has been a dynamic at play in which cloud computing, the Internet of things, and mobile computing were added to the mix. This created enormous diversity of computing solutions and thus unprecedented challenges and opportunities for performance design and analysis. It is important to understand the impact of both consolidation and distribution upon performance. Neither "style" will provide all the answers.

A CONSOLIDATION STUDY

This will examine 144 servers and their utilization. Here are the distributions of utilization on the servers:

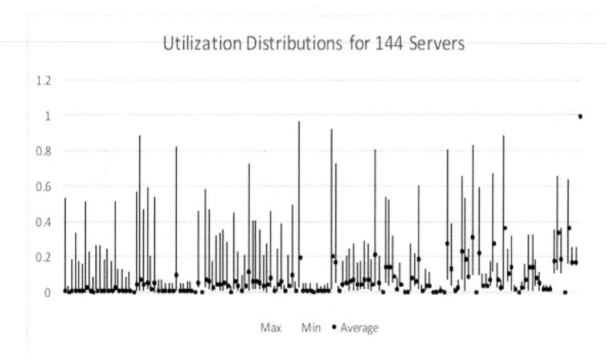

The average utilization is the small black box on each line. Notice how low the averages are. Almost all of the deviation from the average is in the upper tails, and is often quite large. This is an indication of fat and long upper tails and bursty loads.

Recall that the Coefficient of Variability is defined as the Standard Deviation / Average:

$$c = \frac{s}{m}$$

Recall that Rogers' Equation relates c to Uavg and kmax.

$$u_{avg} = \frac{1}{1 + k_{max}c}$$

Recall our definition of Relative Headroom.

$$HR_{avg} = k_{max}c$$

It can also be shown that the HR(u) at any value of utilization u is

$$HR(u) = \frac{1 - u}{u}$$

Plotting Uavg v HRavg for our 144 servers we get:

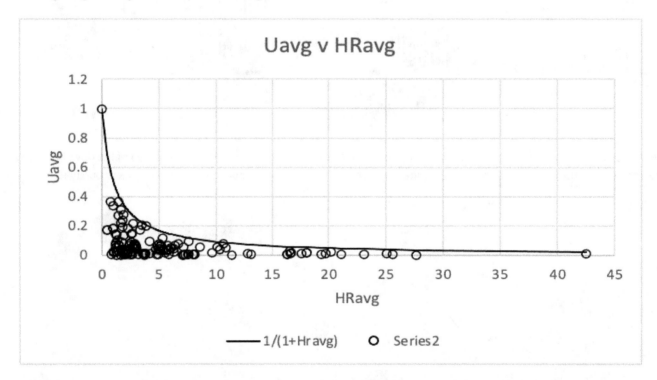

Utilization has an inverse relationship with HR. Since the maximum peak is 1, then 1/(1+HR) is the upper bound on average utilization. If the peak is at less than 1, the average utilization will fall below the line. Here, it is very clear that based on average utilization, many of these servers will have ETR well below their ITR. Part of the shortfall is due to the measurement of utilization as an average over time. Umax must reach 1 to put the measurement on the line. Plotting k and c v HRavg for our servers, we get the following chart.

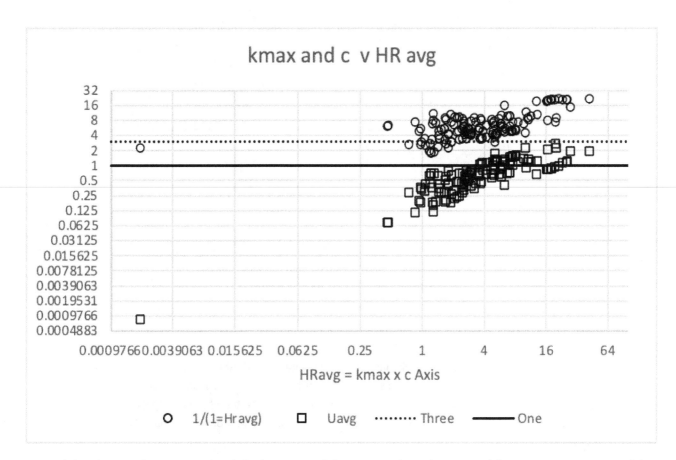

kmax and c v HR avg

HRavg = kmax x c Axis

○ 1/(1=Hr avg) □ Uavg ········ Three ── One

In normal distributions, k =3 is considered the beginning of the upper tail. Moderate variability is at c = 1. For most of these servers, kmax is well above 3, and c is well below 1. High k with low c is an indicator of a bursty load driving high spikes but averaging low utilization. This is one of the sources of Low ETR/ITR on distributed servers and a driver of the emergence of virtualization in the early 2000s. Plotting c v k_{max} we get:

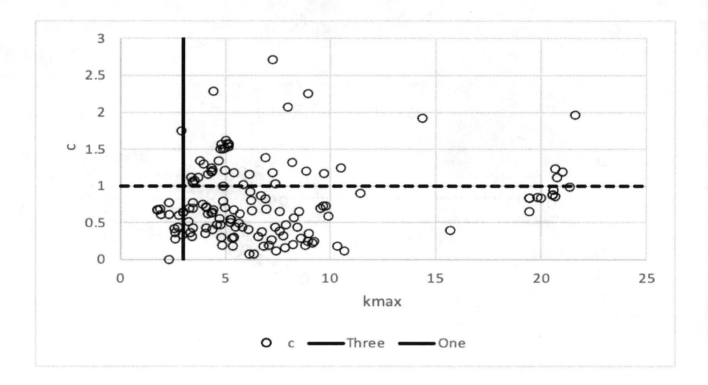

Points with k < 3 are to the left of the vertical line. These servers may have distributions that approach normal distributions. Points with c < 1 are below the horizontal line. These servers have distributions with low variability. Points to the right of k = 3 and below c = 1 are bursty loads. These loads show low variability most of the time but have spikes of high utilization and temporarily have high variability near the spikes. Points to the right of k = 3 and above c =1 have high variability and low average utilization.

The points to the right of k = 3 have fat and/or long upper tails. This drives a need to be conservative in attempting to drive ETR toward ITR. The relatively high probability of large deviations makes response time issues more likely as the utilization increases. For this type of usage pattern, it is best to design for kmax much greater than k = 3.

For the bursty distributions, it becomes necessary to look at the intervals near the bursts and ignore the long intervals of low utilization when determining the utilization statistics from the data. This will avoid underestimating c and k, as they make a difference to the user experience. The alternative is to use very high k, which results in low average utilization.

Here is a plot of a bursty workload time series.

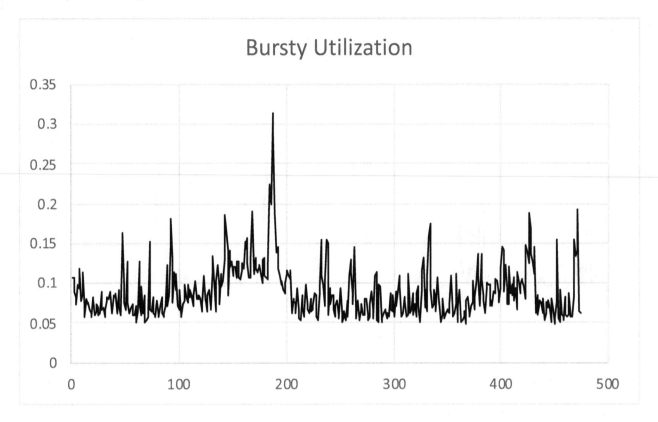

- The average utilization is low: Uavg = 0.172

- Umax is also quite low: Umax = 0.251

- The standard deviation is low: Stdev = 0.013

- C is low: c = 0.074

- kmax is high: kmax = 6.14

High k with low c is an indication of a bursty load.

Here is how c varies over time. We plot a running average of c based on three 15-minute intervals every 15 **minutes.**

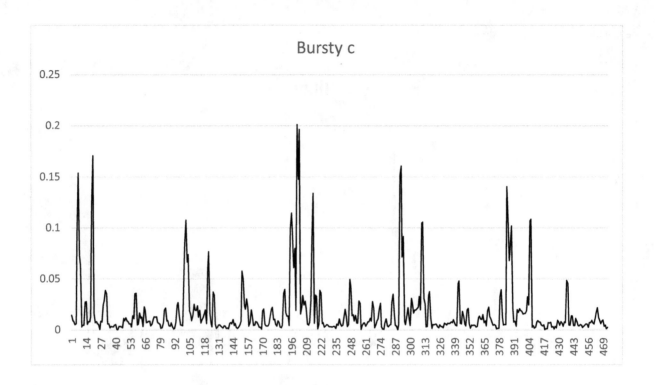

Notice that c reaches nearly 1.7 during the time near the highest spike of utilization. These are the periods that matter.

Here are the statistics for the peak 45 minutes:

- The average utilization is higher but still low: $U_{avg} = 0.208$

- c is higher: $c = 0.178$

- k is much lower: $k_{max} = 1.15$

- $U_{max} = 0.251$

- Stdev = 0.0370

For bursty loads, we must design for the peak and average of busy periods rather than the peak and average of the entire set of intervals.

The ETR for bursty loads will always be low because the high HR requirement drives Uavg down.

CONSOLIDATION

Part of the problem comes from the very nature of distributed systems. It turns out that the variability of the load decreases with consolidation and increases with distribution. Recall Rogers' equation:

$$U_{avg} = 1/(1 + k_{max}c)$$

If we distribute a piece of work on s servers, this becomes:

$$u_{avg} = 1/(1 + k_{max}cs^{1/2})$$

This assumes that the work on the original server is divided evenly among the s identical servers. It is the same as saying that c gets larger when we distribute loads. If distribution pushes c above 1, the operation moves into the lower left quadrant of the UPI v Utilization chart.

If, on the other hand, we have n identical server loads that we put on one server, the equation becomes:

$$u_{avg} = 1/(1 + k_{ma}n^{-1/2})$$

This is the same as saying that the c gets smaller when loads are consolidated and larger when loads are distributed. When c is below 1, the operation moves into the preferred quadrant of our UPI v Utilization chart.

In reality, most of the loads to be consolidated are not identical nor are the servers that they run on. While it is possible to work this out analytically for loads with normal independently random distributions, there is usually some correlation due to interactions and the nature of the workday. Also, as we have seen, utilization distributions are rarely normal. Thus, any analytic solution like Rogers' equation is an estimate.

The effect of consolidation on adding the utilization data on an interval-by-interval basis unfolds as each server is added. The first thing we have to do is to convert each server utilization into a common throughput metric. This can be an ITR metric, which we multiply by the utilization values to get an ETR estimate for each interval. We will use our "clock times cores" estimator. This is not the best ITR metric, but it will suffice.

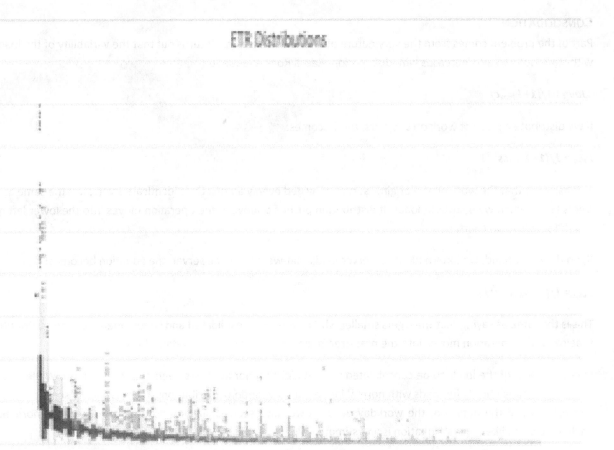

We start by scaling the utilization data for each of the 144 servers by its MHz rating.

The next step is to analyze the sum of all the interval data and discover the peak interval of the sum and the individual server contributions to that peak. We then order the server data from the highest contribution to the lowest contribution, starting with a single server, which is the largest contributor. The next column contains the first server data plus the data for the next highest contributor. This is repeated until the last column contains the consolidation of all 144 servers in our study.

Here is the box chart of the progressive consolidation distributions. Notice that there are still whiskers indicating a fat tail, but they are much shorter than the unconsolidated data.

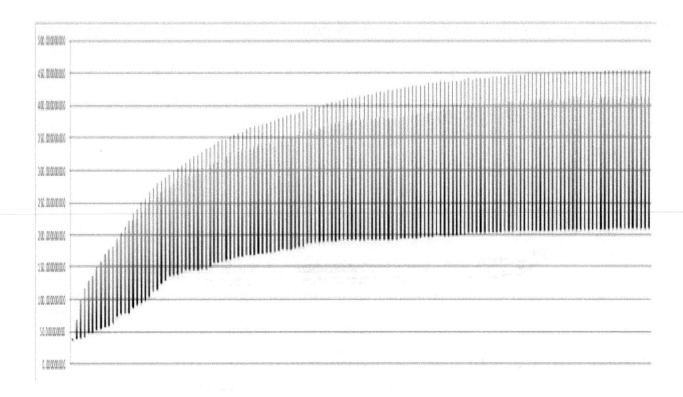

Consolidation reduces variability, allowing ETR to approach ITR.

From the performance point of view, the primary reason for consolidated loads is to reduce c, allowing ETR to rise at a decent response time. It allows the UPI v Utilization curve to show operation in the upper-right quadrant, where both utilization and UPI are > 0.5.

The reduction of c for this workload is not as it would have been estimated by Rogers' equation. In this case, the machine with the largest contribution to the peak runs "hot" throughout the whole measurement period and therefore has very, very low c as an initial value. The variability climbs until about five servers are consolidated, and then c begins its inverse slope. Notice that all these consolidations would run in the "preferred quadrant" for ITR and response time.

Here is the plot if we leave off the first server from the consolidation.

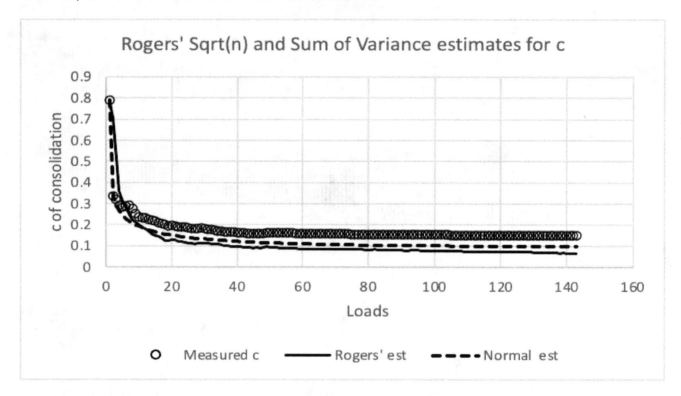

Using Rogers' equation, a variability estimate is calculated by dividing the average c of the individual servers by the square root of the number of servers consolidated (horizontal axis). Assuming normal distribution shows another estimate: c = sqrt(sum of variances)/(sum of averages). Thus, we can say that consolidating 100 servers will cause a reduction in variability that approaches tenfold. We can also say that the variance of the consolidated load will approach the sum of the variances of the distributed load. Dividing by the sum of the averages estimates c. Since utilization distributions are rarely normal and loads are rarely totally uncorrelated, these estimates are optimistic.

Rogers' equation and sum of variance estimates form lower bounds for variability.

Here is the time series utilization plot of the consolidation with varying interval sizes. The chart shows utilization values with a raw data maximum of 75% utilization of the large machine at fifteen-minute intervals.

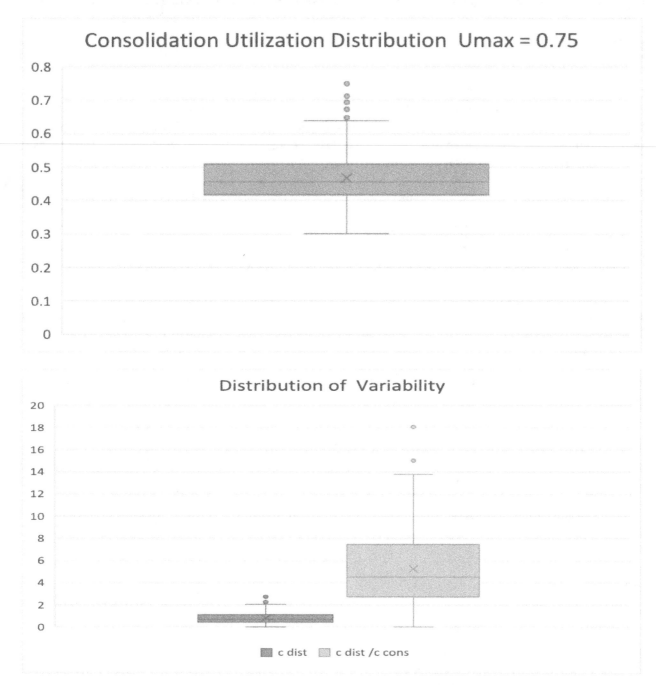

The consolidated load is more nearly normal than most of the distributed servers. There are a few outliers causing a fat upper tail. However, k(100) ~5 contains the load. This average utilization is near 50%. The variability improvement varies from 2 to 18, except for the hot server mentioned above, which runs at near 100% utilization all the time. This server accounts for the lower tail reaching zero.

Part 6: Transition: CPU Intense to Nest Intense Performance

Consolidating loads affects more than the core utilization. Each server's workload uses memory space and cache space. Memory and cache space utilization is less variable than core utilization. As a result, consolidation of workloads causes average cache and memory usage to grow faster than core usage. Eventually, the cache miss rate increases and the memory and cache miss (nest) delays increase. Paging (swapping) starts to occur. This reduces scaling and thread speed, causing the machine to saturate at lower utilization. These effects eventually cause a transition from being CPU/thread bound to being memory/cache bound.

Large "enterprise" class servers such as IBM Power 9 and Oracle SPARC M Series, as well as IBM System z mainframes, have significantly more cache and/or memory than two-socket Oracle T-series, Intel servers, MIPS, or ARM servers. Four- and eight-socket Intel servers can contain very large memory. Enterprise-class servers also have more I/O connections and bandwidth. As a result, enterprise-class servers can consolidate more workloads per CPU than the mass-produced two- socket servers used in distributed clusters and most major public cloud offerings.

This defines another metric, which we call "capacity" C_N. We use the size of the highest-level cache as an estimator.

We often set C_N to 1 for a base machine or the largest machine in a group to be compared. In the former case, all machines with more cache than the base machine will have $C_N > 1$. In the latter case, all machines will have a $C_N <= 1$. One could use total memory or some more sophisticated measurement for C_N but total cache seems to drive enough insight and differentiation, particularly for planning, design, and analysis.

Related to C_N is thread capacity, C_T.

$$C_T = C_N S_T / Threads$$

This defines the ability of a machine to stack work on a single thread, which depends on both the cache/thread and threads speed.

SUMMARY OF PERFORMANCE METRICS

ITR – This is a benchmarked result that measures ITR = Threads x Thread Speed. The estimator is:

ITR ~ Clock Rate x Cores

(We also have a way to estimate the impact of multithreaded cores on ITR.)

ETR – This represents the owners' view of performance. It is aligned with business value.

ETR = ITR x f(u). The estimator is: ETR(u) ~ ITR x u

Average ETR < ITR

Tr – Response Time is the users' view of performance Tr = Ts + Tw. The estimator is UPI:

$$UPI = \frac{T_s}{T_r} \cong \frac{1}{1 + \frac{c^2 u}{1 - u}}$$

C_N – the capacity to hold data close to the processor cores is a proxy for the number of normalized virtual machines, users, processes, or programs the machine can contain.

$$C_N \sim Total\ High\ Level\ Cache$$

C_T – the ability of a single thread to handle stacked work

$$C_T = \frac{C_N S_T}{Threads}$$

Since thread speed = ITR/Threads:

$$C_T = \frac{C_N ITR}{Threads^2}$$

When thread capacity is important, thread count is a liability. This is especially true when ITR(p) < p x ITR(1). Capacity is often normalized by defining a representative machine as having $C_N = 1$

Part 7: Scaling and Saturation

Up until now, we have assumed that ETR is well represented by the estimator.

ETR ~ u ITR, which implies that u ~ ETR/ITR.

ETR approaches u ITR in workloads that do not put pressure on the metric "N." However, as workloads demand more memory and/or cache per core, ETR drops below what the estimator predicts. Not only does this reduce the initial thread speed but also causes additional slowdown as the load is increased. While Little's law remains a simple linear statement of thread speed times threads, thread speed decreases with load size, causing ETR(u) and ETR(p) to increase sublinearly. A consequence of this is that Cn and Ct increase in importance for loads that behave this way. The growth of ITR when resources (particularly processors) are added is known as scaling.

ETR increases sublinearly with utilization. This is known as a saturation curve

$$ETR = f(u)ITR$$

Where $\frac{f(u)}{u} \leq 1$

We know that:
$$u(p) = \frac{p_{Busy}}{p}$$

Since ITR is defined as the case : $p_{busy}/p \rightarrow 1$

$$ETR\left(\frac{p_{Busy}}{p}\right) \sim ITR(p_{Busy})$$

This is a property of any valid f(u). It is called the duality of saturation and scaling. We will come to rely on it. Duality means that the saturation curve of a multiprocessor system is approximately the same as the scaling curve. It follows that a load that causes saturation also causes sublinear scaling as the core count increases. ETR is expressed as an estimator here. We know that utilization is a statistic and is measured as an average. For any interval of time, the utilization can be measured from cores that vary in utilization. Thus, during any interval, any instance of p_{busy}/p can be either higher or lower than the measured u for the interval.

ETR for a machine using p cores is approximately the ITR of a machine with p cores.

MODELS FOR SCALING F(P) AND SATURATION F(U)

Models for the scaling of ITR or the saturation of ETR describe how the data changes as p(p_{Busy}) is increased from 1 to a maximum value. Because of duality, the models are the same.

Our Clock x Cores throughput estimator has linear scaling. That is, the scaling curve is a straight line.

$$ITR(p) \sim (Clk)(p)$$

$$ETR(p) \sim (ITR)(u) = (Clk)(p)(u) = (Clk)\left(\frac{p_{Busy}}{p}\right)(p) = (Clk)(p_{Busy})$$

Both models are straight lines with slope "Clk." Notice that duality property is preserved.

In reality, most multiprocessor systems show sublinear scaling. To refine our estimators we need sublinear scaling models. We start applying duality to the fundamentals of performance from the Owner and User perspectives.

Throughput: $\quad ETR\left(\frac{p_{Busy}}{p}\right) = ITR(p_{Busy})$

Response Time: $\quad \dfrac{1}{ITR(p_{Busy})} \leq T_r(p_{Busy}) \leq \dfrac{p_{Busy}}{ITR(p_{Busy})}$

To model scalability, we need to measure throughput for multiple values of p_{usy}. Recalling that *ITR is **always** threads x thread speed and assuming single-threaded cores,* we get:

Thread Speed: $\quad S_t = \dfrac{1}{T_r(p_{Busy})} = \dfrac{ITR(p_{Busy})}{p_{Busy}}$

From here on we will indicate pBusy with p if we are using ITR data to establish processor scaling and n when something else (users, connections, tasks, etc.) is scaling. This is customary.

We start with the following definitions of Relative ITR and Relative T_r

$$RITR(p) \equiv \frac{ITR(p)}{ITR(1)}$$

$$RTR(p) \equiv \frac{p}{RITR(p)}$$

Most scaling models take the form:

$$RITR(p) = \frac{p}{RT_r(p)}$$

The numerator is the independent variable p. It is a positive integer and precisely known when using ITR data to represent processor scaling. In theory, the denominator is a polynomial. Sometimes p is a constant and another scaling factor is used such as users, messages, packets, files, jobs, connections, etc. We can use the same scaling models. In this case we conventionally replace p with "n" or another indexing symbol.

$$RT_r(p) = Ap^2 + Bp + C \ (Quadratic \ form)$$

Depending on the coefficients, there are 4 cases:

1. $RT_r(p) = C \ (Constant)$
2. $RT_r(p) = Bp + C \ (Linear)$
3. $RT_r(p) = Ap^2 + Bp + C \ (Quadratic)$
4. $RT_r(p) = Ap^2 - Ap + C \ (Quadratic)$

By definition: $RITR(p) \equiv \frac{ITR(p)}{ITR(1)} \rightarrow RITR(1) \equiv 1$

For the common scaling models: Linear, Amdahl, USL, and Contention Free USL, C is set to 1. For scaling, the scaling unit (p,n) count is a given and independent variable. We can collect ITR data for various unit counts and determine the model that fits best by doing regression using the quadratic form. We can then build a model for ITR(p) and extrapolate and/or interpolate to generate data for unmeasured points.

Before we do this, we must first look at the actual models to determine how each model constrains the coefficients. Most models express this as a ratio of ITR(p) to ITR(1), called RITR(p), which is also known as "speedup" or "relative capacity."

By definition:

RITR(p) = ITR(p)/ITR(1)

We can use this equation to establish scaling using RITR(p) and then generate ITR(P) by multiplying by ITR(1). Duality lets us use ITR. Thus utilization is at or near 100%, and service time is a constant. Since service time is fixed, taking the ratio to get ITR cancels it out. Therefore:

$1/RITR(p) <= RT_R <= p/RITR(p)$

$1/RITR$ is called **RPT_r**. This is the relative response time if the unit of work uses all the processors in parallel. **p/RITR** is also called **RST_r**. This is the response time if the unit of work uses a single-threaded core.

For single-threaded cores **$1/RST_R = RS_T$**. By Little's law, **$RITR(p) = p \times RS_T$**. This implies that **$RITR(p) = p/RST_r(p)$**. Most of the scaling models are based on this.

The common models all set **$RT_R = RST_r$**.

The common models are:

Linear Scaling:

$$RITR(p) = p \;\rightarrow\; RT_r(p) = 1 \rightarrow RT_r(p) = \frac{1}{ITR(1)} \;\rightarrow\; RITR(p) = RITR(1)p$$

Amdahl's Law:

$$RITR(p) = \frac{p}{1+\sigma(p-1)} \rightarrow RT_r(p) = 1 + \sigma(p-1)$$

Gunther's USL:

$$ITR(p) = \frac{p}{1+\sigma(p-1)+\kappa p(p-1)} \rightarrow RT_r(p) = 1 + (\sigma - \kappa)(p-1) + \kappa(p-1)^2$$

Sigma = 0 Law:

$$RITR(p) = \frac{p}{1 - \kappa(p-1) + \kappa p(p-1)} \rightarrow RT_r(p) = 1 - \kappa(p-1) + \kappa(p-1)^2$$

There is a fifth scaling law that was derived separately and does not easily fit the quadratic form.

Gustafson's Law:

$$RITR(p) = s + (1-s)p \rightarrow RT_r = \frac{p}{s+(1-s)p} \rightarrow PRT_r = \frac{1}{s+(1-s)p}$$

Gustafson's law is applied to "shared nothing" systems like supercomputers running in SPMD mode and clusters of distributed computers working collaboratively or on largely independent loads. It works because the workload scales with the infrastructure and because contention is much lower in these machines than happens when processors share memory.

This gives rise to the idea of a contention free form of the USL, which we call the Sigma = 0 Law. This will approach Gustafson's law for small kappa. As kappa grows it will provide a more accurate view of scaling than Gustafson's law.

We can use the equation for Gunther's USL for all but the Gustafson scaling law. The physical interpretation of the models is as follows:

Sigma is the amount of serialization of load due to "contention" for shared resources. A good example is a contention that occurs when multiple processors contend for shared memory or multiple programs contend for a variable or file.

Kappa is the amount of cross-talk, coherence, or communication traffic delay between the entities that are scaling. Examples are the internode communication traffic in a cluster or supercomputer that cannot be overlapped with execution, causing programs or processors to enter I/O wait states. In shared-memory multiprocessors, this can be the traffic between caches that occurs when a single memory location that is cached in more than one place is modified. The equation is $p(p-1)$ rather than $(p-1)^2$ because the traffic is a function of the logical interconnections between the processors rather than the processor count.

Summary of Scaling Modes and Regression

We can collect ITR data for various processor counts and determine the model that fits best by doing "regression." Regression is a mathematical way to "fit" data to a curve represented by an equation. For our models above, regression will give us values for A, B, and C or the RTr(p) quadratic. We will find kappa and sigma as combinations of the coefficients. We can then build the model ITR(p) = p/RTr(p). Regression routines are available in many programming platforms, like R and Python. However, for regression of a quadratic form, we can work directly with the data using a polynomial trendline feature in the Microsoft Excel x-y scatter graphs. Once we have A, B, and C, we can also extrapolate and interpolate to scaling points that we haven't measured

ABC:

$$RT_r(p) = (1 - \sigma) + (\sigma - \kappa)p + \kappa p^2$$

$$C = 1 - \sigma \quad B = (\sigma - \kappa) \quad A = \kappa \rightarrow B = 1 - C - A \rightarrow A + B + C = 1$$

AB1:

$$RT_r(p) = 1 + (\sigma + \kappa)(p - 1) + \kappa(p - 1)^2$$

$$C = 1 \quad B = \sigma + k \quad A = \kappa \rightarrow \sigma = B - A \quad \kappa = A$$

Sig0 Law:

$$RT_r(p) = 1 - \kappa p + \kappa p^2$$

$$RT_r(p) = 1 + \kappa p(p - 1)$$

Then per Gunther:

$$RT_r(p) = 1 + \sigma(p - 1) + \kappa p(p - 1)$$

Reverts to linear model when $\kappa = 0$ and $\sigma = 0$ and to Amdahl's Law when $\kappa = 0$ and $\sigma > 0$. When $\kappa > 0$ and $\sigma = 0$ this becomes Sig0 law.

Derivation of USL Parameter Values:

$$RT_r(p) = 1 + \sigma(p-1) + \kappa p(p-1)$$

$$RT_r(X) = 1 + \sigma X + \kappa(X+1)(X)$$

$$RT_r(X) = 1 + (\sigma + \kappa)(X) + \kappa X^2$$

The regression equation for generating the parameters is:

$$RT_r(p) = A(p-1)^2 + B(p-1) + 1 \text{ (The AB1 model)}$$

In Excel this is the 2nd order polynomial trend line equation with the y intercept set to one. Excel will generate this upon request on an x-y scatter plot.

$$RT_r(p) = 1 + \sigma(p-1) + \kappa p(p-1) \rightarrow RT_r(p) = 1 + (B-A)p + Ap(p-1)$$

$$RT_r(X) = 1 + \sigma X + \kappa(X+1)(X)$$

$$RT_r(X) = 1 + (\sigma + \kappa)(X) + \kappa X^2$$

$$A = \kappa \quad B = \sigma + A \rightarrow \sigma = B - A \text{ so:}$$

$$RT_r(p) = 1 + (B-A)p + Ap(p-1) \text{ (The USL Model)}$$

THE COMMON MODELS

We present the scaling profile charts for various scaling cases. The charts plot three curves: RITR(p), its inverse PRTr, RSt, and its inverse RTr.

LINEAR MODEL

This is the model for our ITR = Clk x Cores model. It represents "perfect" scaling and assumes that all threads run without any interaction with other threads.

RITR(p) = p

RTr(p) = 1

Here is the resulting scaling profile:

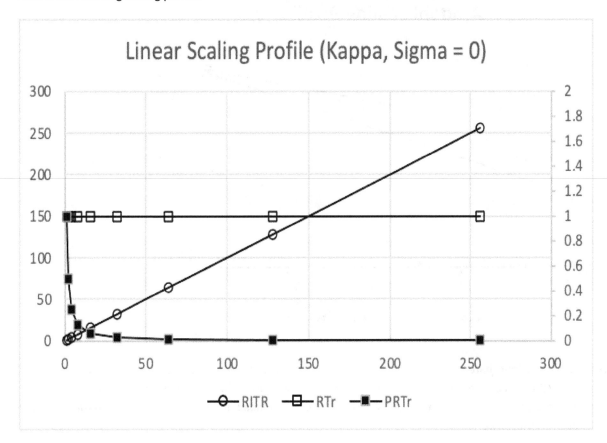

AMDAHL'S LAW

Gene Amdahl of IBM initially argued that programs contain at least some serial content, which causes sublinear scaling. He argued that a role remains for large, single-processor machines. While multiprocessing is the standard today, the serial content of loads certainly puts limits on the use of the many slow cores to replace a set of faster cores.

The law is expressed as:

$$RITR(p) = \frac{p}{1 + \sigma(p-1)}$$

$$RTr(p) = 1 + \sigma(p-1)$$

The law has one parameter, sigma, which represents the fraction of the load that must be serialized. Here is the scaling profile for sigma = 0.01

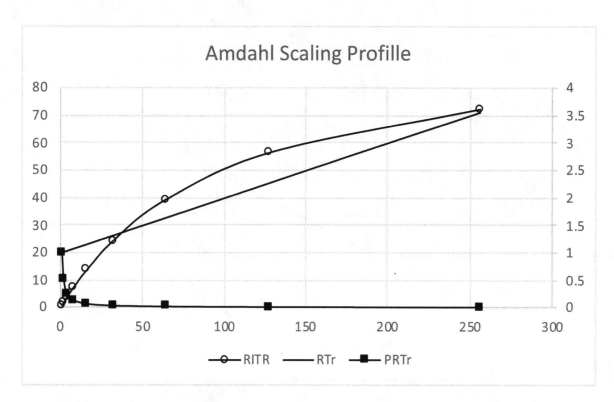

Amdahl Scaling Profille

In multiprocessing systems that share memory, sigma usually shows up as contention for shared resources such as threads, cache, memory, and I/O interfaces. In software, it occurs when a variable must be locked and allocated to a single program so that it can be updated coherently. Serialization can also occur when a workload manager, transaction monitor, scheduler, or database manager prioritizes work.

For large p:

$$RITR\,(p) \rightarrow \frac{1}{\sigma}$$

$$RT_r(p) \rightarrow \infty$$

The slope of the RTr is sigma:

$$\frac{dRT_r(p)}{dp} = \sigma$$

The value of Amdahl's law is that it is derived from a primary source of serialization, which is the load itself. Programs and multiprogramming loads are never completely parallel. This is due to the nature of programming: Algorithms and their underlying mathematics are made up of sequential steps. A program can be replicated to run in parallel on multiple processors, but the underlying algorithm takes multiple steps to complete.

There are no completely parallel programs. Completely sequential loads are rare.

GUNTHER'S UNIVERSAL SCALING LAW (USL) – AMDAHL WAS AN OPTIMIST

Amdahl's law was developed at the beginning of the minicomputer era (ca 1970). It explained why the mainframe would not immediately be replaced by clusters of minicomputers. Subsequently, scaling grew significantly, and parallel computing was being applied to machines that contained a significant amount of cache memory. Initially, caches were private to each core. One consequence of these developments was that IT solutions now had to deal with maintaining the coherence of multiple copies of data held in various places with the "nest" and/or the "network." The resulting "coherence traffic" or "crosstalk" between caches, memories, other nodes, and disk drives reduced thread speed. Gunther improved on Amdahl's scaling model by adding a second parameter called kappa. Kappa represents the impact of coherence traffic on scaling.

$$RITR(p) = \frac{p}{1 + \sigma(p-1) + \kappa(p)(p-1)}$$

$$RT_r(p) = 1 + \sigma(p-1) + \kappa(p)(p-1)$$

If we keep sigma = 0.01 and set ka, ,

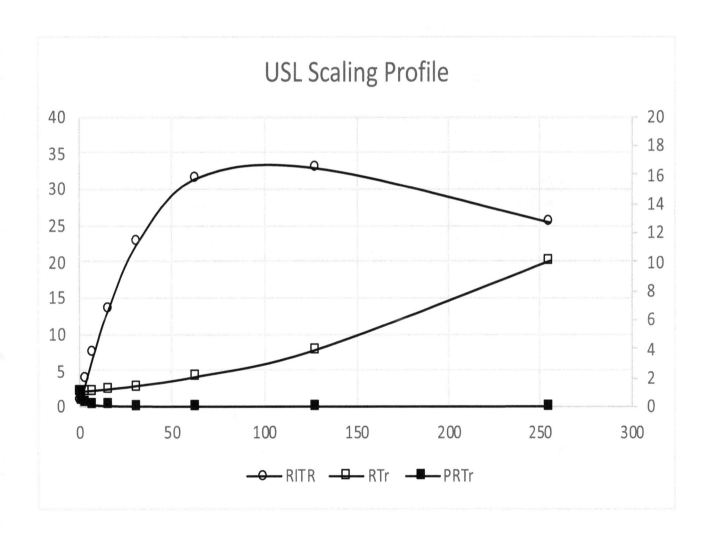

This model has the following properties.

A maximum occurs:

$$p_{max} = Integer\left(\sqrt{(1-\sigma)/\kappa}\right)$$

Per Gunther the properties are as follows:

pmax → 0 as kappa → Infinity

pmax → Infinity as kappa → 0

pmax → kappa$^{-1/2}$ as sigma → 0

pmax → 1 as sigma → 1

USING THE AB1 MODEL REGRESSION TO DETERMINE THE MAXIMUM

AB1 regression parameters were constrained such that:

$$A = \kappa \quad B = \sigma - \kappa \quad C = 1$$

This means that: $p_{max} = Integer\left(\sqrt{\frac{1-(B+A)}{A}}\right)$

GUSTAFSON SCALING – AMDAHL AND GUNTHER WERE PESSIMISTS

The math of Amdahl's law and Gunther's extensions assumes that scaling is all about speed for a given problem size. Gustafson argued that scaling is better when the size of the problem is allowed to grow along with the resources. Amdahl asked, "How much faster will this piece of work get done if more cores are applied?" Gustafson asked, "How much more work can be done in the same amount of time if more cores are applied?" The change of question changes the math, and the scaling gets better.

Gustafson defined scaling as:

$$RITR = s + (1-s)p$$

$$RT_r = \frac{p}{s + (1-s)p} = \frac{1}{s/p + p - sp}$$

This results in the following scaling profile:

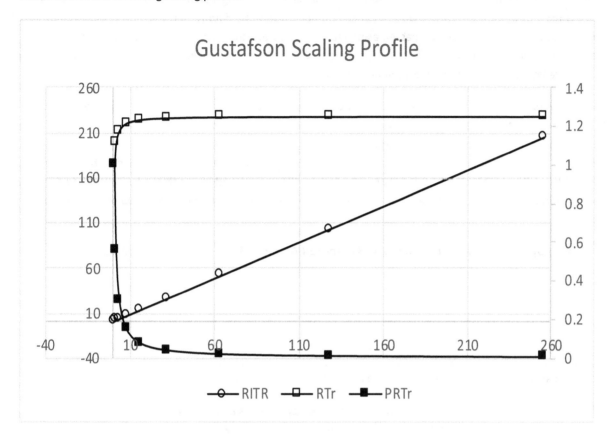

In this model:

RITR grows linearly with a slope of 1-s

RTr rapidly approaches an asymptote of 1/1-s

Notice that we show larger values of s than for Amdahl's sigma. This is because Gustafson pushes programming parallelism to the limit of the underlying algorithm. The primary application of this scaling model is for grid, cluster, and supercomputer solutions. Their workloads are often worked on with a divide-and-conquer strategy. Workloads that have little thread interaction have very low s; they are often called "embarrassingly parallel" and they scale extremely well. Other workloads require a larger common serial algorithm to be run.

Shared-nothing architectures, grids, and clusters of computing nodes are interconnected by switches and/or network connections. These configurations reach very high levels of scaling. Most of their work has thread interaction/communication that is significantly higher than embarrassingly parallel applications but significantly lower than the transaction, database, and multi-tenant workload run on large multiprocessors with shared memory (aka SMPs). The amount of communication is modeled by increasing s depending on the amount of communication required. That is, communication is considered part of the serialized work. While it does not force sublinear scaling as in Amdahl's law, thread interaction can lead to large s. In extreme cases, this will break the model. When this happens, the work is usually inappropriate for parallel computing.

Gustafson scaling is mainly used to describe how clusters or networks of computers can scale to do large, numerically intense workloads. These networks are known as massively parallel processors (MPPs) or parallel supercomputers, or grid clusters. They don't explicitly share memory but generally have some form of message passing interface (MPI) protocol. A divide-and-conquer strategy is used to put a "cell" of the work on each computer. Only the data required at the cell boundaries are communicated between nodes. These data are passed as messages. In clusters, the messages travel on network packets. In supercomputers a lightweight protocol over high-scale, high-speed switches is used for the internode communication in order to reduce the message latency that is inherent in standard network protocols.

Modern high-end servers can contain as many as or more processing cores than the original parallel supercomputers and clusters had. Their nests are far more complex than a shared interface to memory that the original scaling models were designed for. There is a certain amount of Gustafson scaling involved in building workloads to fill large, shared memory processors. Also, such processors are often partitioned into virtual machines, containers, or physical nodes that behave like clusters or even MPPs. Message passing systems share memory in I/O buffers and network hardware. Shared memory systems pass semaphores, lock protocols, and interrupts between software modules; shared memory is often used to contain message data.

All Message Passing Systems Share Some Memory; All Shared Memory Systems Pass Some Messages

The art of parallel computing has 10 main ideas:

1. Understanding how to partition work onto multiple threads and the use of redundant execution to reduce thread interaction
2. Understanding how to partition data to minimize sharing and contention
3. Understanding how to build efficient communication protocols between the partitions (granularity, overhead, and processing/IO overlap)
4. Understanding how to manage locking mechanisms when resources are shared
5. Understanding the underlying infrastructure and the balance of thread, nest, and I/O resources
6. Understanding the uses of SIMD, SPMD, and MIMD software paradigms and their combinations
7. Understanding how nest Intensity affects scaling in parallel systems
8. Understanding pinning and locality of reference in parallel systems
9. Understanding storage and memory sharing in multi-node systems
10. Understanding how workload impacts exploitation of parallelism

SIGMA = 0 – GUSTAFSON WAS AN OPTIMIST

Gustafson's scaling law was meant to explain the behavior of "shared nothing" systems in which each program has its own processor and memory resources. Collaboration in such systems is handled through communication using network I/O. In terms of the USL, these systems can be modeled with sigma = 0 and positive kappa. Given the relationship of kappa and sigma to the regression parameters, the zero sigma model is:

$$RT_r(p) = \kappa(p-1)^2 - \kappa(p-1) + 1$$

$$RITR(p) = \frac{(p)}{\kappa(p-1)^2 - \kappa(p-1) + 1}$$

For sufficiently small kappa, this model approaches the Gustafson scaling profile.

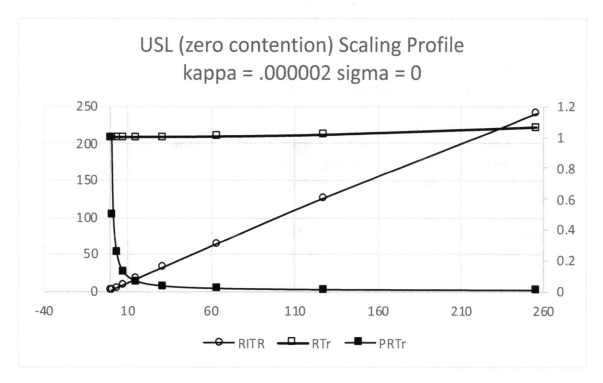

The USL can provide a more realistic scaling model than Gustafson, particularly when shared-nothing nodes become shared-data nodes and the shared data is modified.

That is, as the threads interact more in a shared-nothing environment, kappa grows. Sigma can be estimated at zero because contention when communicating is usually small compared to contention for shared memory. Like many USL models, the Sig0 model will reach a maximum scale point. Because sigma = 0, the maximum pmax = sqrt(1/kappa). In this case pmax = 707.

Here is what happens when kappa grows sufficiently to cause retrograde scaling in the range that we are considering:

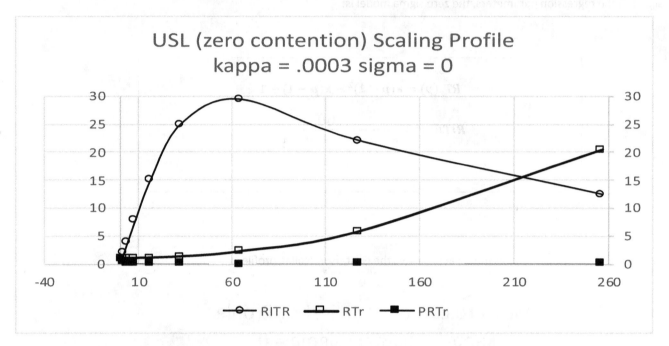

You can see that at kappa = 0.0003, the maximum moves back to 57. When sigma = 0, the initial scaling is very nearly linear.

KAPPA < 0 – AMDAHL AND GUNTHER WERE PESSIMISTS

Gunther saw no meaning in negative kappa and asserted that if negative kappa is measured, the data must be in error. Modern shared-memory multiprocessor systems often exhibit negative kappa when their scaling data is fit to the USL. Neither the model nor the large machine's data is faulty in this case. It merely indicates that other resources and/or the load required to fill the machine scale as well as the processors.

Gunther correctly attributed this to non-uniform memory access (NUMA) effects of complex nests. He suggested that we nest USL models around "local memory" to get a clearer answer. This does work, but we will show that the physical structure of the solution at hand will be the principal driver of moving the USL away from data. Sometimes this is revealed as negative kappa.

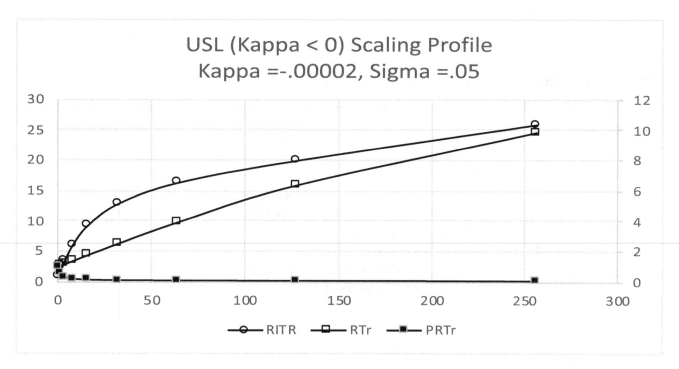

When building a "piecewise" model, physical characteristics almost always drive the pieces to be chosen. However, software constraint relief can also cause the model to underestimate scaling, creating ripples in the data. Here is the scaling profile that results when this happens. Here RTr(p) is convex rather than concave, and the RITR is more gently sublinear particularly at a relatively high scale.

NEGATIVE KAPPA AND VERY HIGH SCALING

We see that RTr is also convex when kappa is negative. The question is, does the slope ever reach zero or turn negative? What does the shape of this curve mean? To examine this we take the derivative (find the slope) of the RTr regression equation.[3]

Let $X = p - 1$

$$RTr(X) = AX^2 + BX + 1$$

Find slope $\qquad\qquad dRTr(X)/dx = 2AX + B$

Set slope to 0 $\qquad\qquad 2AX + B = 0$

Flat slope occurs when $\qquad X = -\dfrac{B}{2A}$

When A is positive, x is negative, and therefore, the result never occurs. When A is negative, x at slope zero is a positive number. Often |A| << B in these instances. The slope typically becomes flat beyond the physical scaling limit of the system being examined.

---

[3] This is the only time that calculus is explicitly used in this book. I tried to avoid it, but there was no good alternative here.

PART 8: SCALING EXAMPLES

In his book *Guerrilla Capacity Planning*, Dr. Gunther lays out the procedure for performing regression on scaling data. In the following example   regression.

THE MODIFIED PROCEDURE.

1. Measure throughput, *ITR*(p), for a set of processor configurations p.
2. Preferably include a p = 1 measurement and at least four others.
3. Calculate the RITR = ITR(p)/ITR(1).
4. Calculate the RTr(p) = p/ITR(p).
5. Use an Excel polynomial (order 2) trend line, setting the intercept to 1, to fit the data displaying the equation of fit.

$$y = Ax^2 + Bx + 1$$

6. Model RT_r(p) and RITR(p)

$$RT_r(p) = A(p-1)^2 + B(p-1) + 1$$

$$RITR(p) = \frac{p}{A(p-1)^2 + B(p-1) + 1}$$

7. Find kappa = A, and sigma = B-A to quantify contention and crosstalk.

A SOFTWARE SCALING EXAMPLE

This is a case that Dr. Gunther used in his text *Guerilla Capacity Planning*.[4] ITR was measured on a web application solution. In this case, software threads are the scaled value. Here is the data.

n	ITR(n)	PTr(n)	Tr(n)	RITR(n)	RPtr(n)	RTr(n)
1	24	0.04166667	0.04166667	1	1	1
2	48	0.02083333	0.04166667	2	0.5	1
4	85	0.01176471	0.04705882	3.54166667	0.28235294	1.12941176
7	100	0.01	0.07	4.16666667	0.24	1.68
10	99	0.01010101	0.1010101	4.125	0.24242424	2.42424242
20	94	0.0106383	0.21276596	3.91666667	0.25531915	5.10638298

The retrograde scaling between 7 and 10 threads indicates significant coherence delay, suggesting that the USL model will do better than the Amdahl and Gustafson models.

ITR(n) is in events per second. Therefore, PTr(n) and Tr(n) are the bounds of the response time in seconds. PTR(n) is 1/ITR(n), the lower bound assuming events occur sequentially and use all the available hardware threads in parallel. Tr(n) is the upper bound and assumes that each event occupies one thread, and multiple events run in parallel. RITR is the throughput normalized to ITR(1) = 1. In this case RITR(n) = ITR(n)/24. Here are the results:

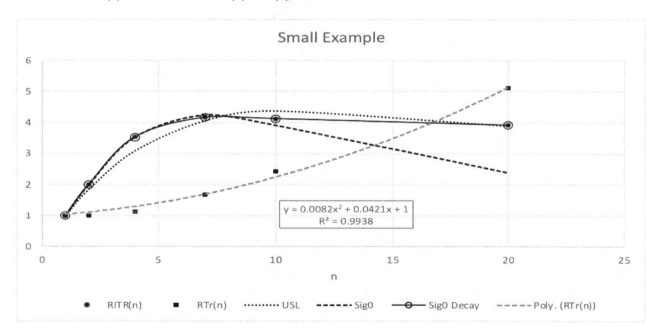

The six data points are the dots labeled RITR(n). The USL model is the dotted line (kappa = 0.0680 sigma = 0.1103). Note that it underestimates the early scaling and overestimates the maximum n. The sigma = 0 model is the dashed line (sigma = 0 and kappa = 0.0155).

---

[4] (Gunther) *Guerilla Capacity Planning*, Chapter 6.7, pp 110-115

This model is better than the standard USL at modeling the early scaling and peak ITR, but significantly underestimates the RITR after retrograde scaling begins. The SigODecay model is the best fit for the data. It uses the Sigma = 0 model for the first five data points and the linear decay for the rest. Normally, moving away from a USL-based model to better fit the data is not a good idea. However, there is good reason to believe that resource saturation is at play in this example. That is, some resource is becoming scarce as the scaling is reaching its peak, limiting scaling and also impacting the behavior of the retrograde scaling.

Here is a RITR(n) v RITR(SIG0Decay) chart that shows the models tracking the data and the best model.

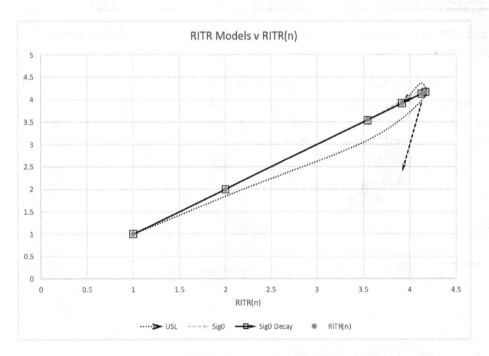

You can see that the Sigma = 0 model tracks the data until retrograde scaling begins; then it becomes pessimistic. The standard USL underestimates RITR(n) until retrograde scaling begins, and then it loops back toward the data. The error is smaller than the error of the Sigma = 0 model during retrograde scaling. This begs the question, "Is a model of the retrograde behavior all that important?" The answer is yes, only if we can tolerate the high response times and/or we have no need for more throughput. In that case, if we accept that the USL breaks down in these overload cases, we can model the decay empirically and from that decide how hard to drive systems.

The plot below is a model of the shape of a classic performance chart called the Response Time v Throughput chart, one of the classic ways to determine the optimal operating point of a system: maximum throughput at low response time. It is built by plotting RTr(n) v RITR(n). Notice the "nose." In this case, the optimal throughput is about four times the unit throughput. The nose comes from the retrograde behavior of the response time at high scale. In this measurement t, the software load was scaled past the optimal throughput of the system.

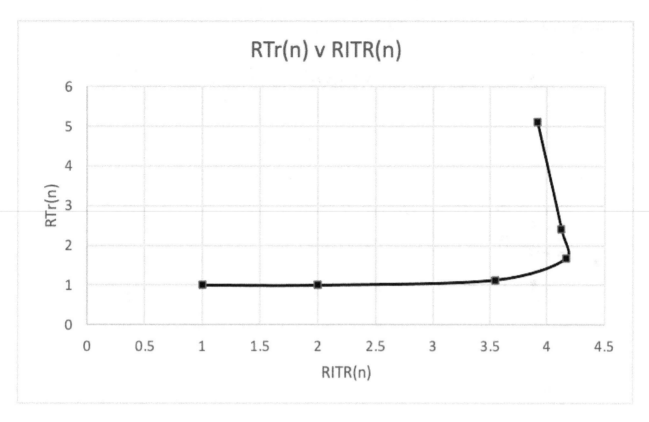

SCALING A CLUSTER OF MIPS PROCESSORS

This is another example from Dr. Gunther's book, *Guerilla Capacity Planning*.

The Silicon Graphics Origin 1000 is a NUMA cluster of MIPS 1000 processors. The processors are connected in a "bristled" hypertorus mesh network. Each bristle is a node containing two MIPS 1000 processors, memory, and connections to an I/O network and the router mesh. The machine in question contains 64 processors which are packaged on four racks, with eight midplane boards, 16 routers, and 32 nodes. Each router can connect to two "local" compute nodes, a router on the same board, a router in the same rack on a second board, a router in an adjacent rack, and a router on a non-adjacent board.

The connection delay from node to node depends on how many connection hops it takes to make the connection. Additional delay is added by each hop. Delays and hop count vary depending on which two nodes are involved in the memory transfer. You can see that for up to four nodes, there are no inter-rack cable connections. Going to two racks (eight nodes) adds four adjacent rack cables that are longer and slower. Going beyond eight nodes adds non-adjacent racks, which are slower yet.

The assumption made in formulating the scaling laws is that the interconnection delay is flat, implying either bus or fully connected switch connections rather than a mesh. This example shows the effects of the mesh connection.

Here is the scaling profile:

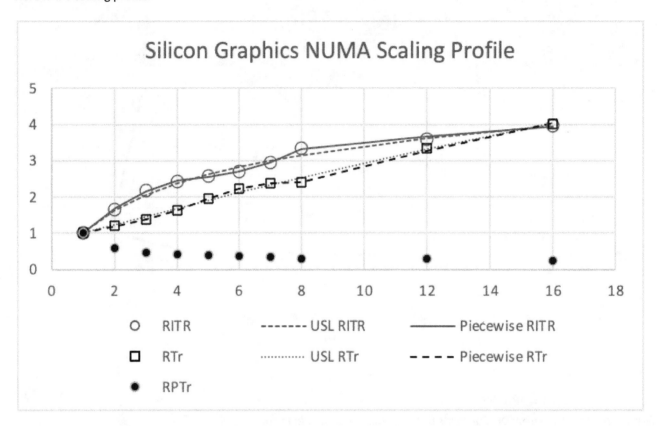

The overall scaling of ITR is not very impressive. Sixteen routers, with four local processors each, yield only four times the ITR. However, the work done on this machine as benchmarked is numerically intense, "ray tracing" graphics code. The data and computing are both easily partitioned to run in parallel. Furthermore, there is more sharing of data between nearest-neighbor partitions, dropping the average hop count in the actual work. This means that the Response Time Unit (RTU) experienced by the users is greater than one thread. We have previously noted that if parallelism can grow with the number of processing units, the users can see RPTr ~ 1/RITR instead of RTr=p/RITr. Often the workload and the code set the amount of parallelism exploited. The RUTr(8) curve sets the RTU to eight threads.

Notice that the USL RTr correlates quite well with the RTr data. Notice also that the convex shape indicates negative kappa. However, the data has a ripple in it relative to the quadratic curve used for the model. Both of these observations indicate that something besides contention and coherence is affecting the scaling. In this case, it is the difference between the physical network interconnecting the processing elements and bus or the fully connected network that is assumed by the models. Here the hypertoroid model of the network causes a nonlinear increase in connection latency as the number of router nodes is increased.

We have calculated the average "hop latency" for 1-8 routers, after normalizing the first router delay to one. We arbitrarily assumed that the "on board" router connections cost 1X and the cable connection costs 2X. Here are the results.

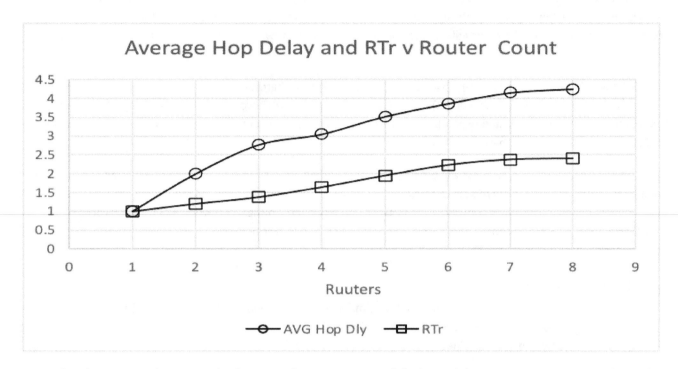

Notice that the same ripple occurs in both curves. The coarse nature of the latency change assumptions causes the ripple in the hop curve to be more pronounced than in the RTR data. Even so, the correlation between the curves is about 96%. It is reasonable to expect that refinement of the latency values with measurements could improve the correlation, leading to an improved model. However, it is not clear whether measuring the latency and building such a model is less effort than simply measuring ITR at every relevant scale point.

Here is the RTr V RITR chart.

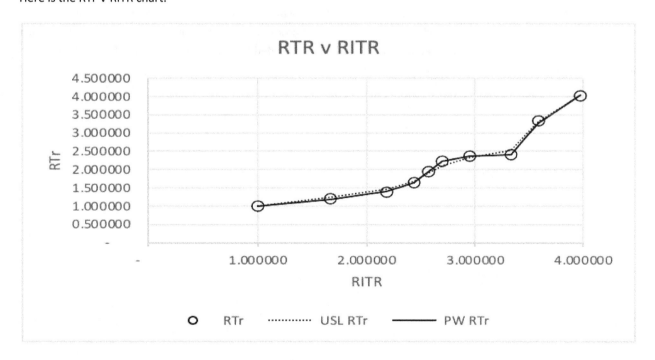

Notice that there is no "nose" in the data, indicating that RITR does not go retrograde before reaching the maximum machine size. This is because the measurements are from a hardware ITR benchmark. The objective of the measurement was to demonstrate the maximum ITR achievable by the hardware. Thus, the software and load were crafted to not overload the system.

We don't have utilization data. However, if we assume the load drives the hardware to its maximum, the utilization is at least approaching 100%. The lack of unbounded RTr growth and/or retrograde RITR would indicate that the load variability is low and that the load has been adjusted to not drive the machine into saturation at utilization <<100%. You can also see that the ripple becomes a surge in this chart.

This is a dated example. Mesh networks are out of favor because they are subject to "orphaned packets" on certain types of routing errors and because they are subject to larger hop counts than other networks. Modern large-scale processors that share memory are built from multi-core CPUs. The CPUs are interconnected by nests of switches and shared cache memories. They exhibit similar ripples, but the shared caches mitigate the multi-hop NUMA effects.

THE IBM Z15 MAINFRAME

IBM provides a full set of core-by-core scaling data for its mainframes. They publish this as the Large Scale Processor Ratios (LSPR). There are various tables for different operating systems and machine vintages. Each table contains core counts and LSPR values for low, medium, and high "nest intensity" (NI) workloads.

NI is a measure of the stress that the workload puts on the nest and its caches. A high NI workload is characterized by high nest traffic, which correlates to relatively low cache hit ratios. On any given machine, low NI workloads scale more linearly than high NI workloads. Machines with lower ITR/cache design ratios scale more linearly than machines with higher ratios.

The mainframe has traditionally had low design ratios because its workload has relatively high NI. Even a low NI LSPR workload has more NI than common CPU benchmarks like SPECint Rate.

Here we examine the scaling of IBM's latest mainframe, the IBM z15. We use the model with four nodes, 16 sockets, and 145 processors here. There is a model with five nodes, 20 sockets, and 190 processors, but it is only available as a whole machine direct from the factory, whereas the four-node machine can be field upgraded from one to four nodes. The following chart shows the scaling difference between low NI and high NI loads.

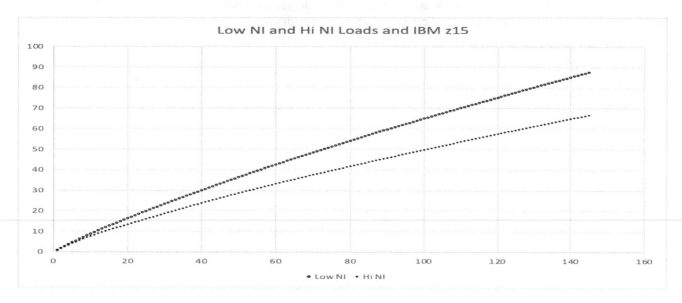

Low NI and Hi NI Loads and IBM z15

High NI loads drive the nest and shared caches harder than low NI loads. As a result, the high NI thread speed is slower due to cache misses. This causes more bend in the scaling curve. Even so, the scaling is very good to a the maximum scale of 145 processors.

We have a similar problem with modeling the scaling for this machine as we did for Silicon Graphics. There is a ripple in the data relative to the USL quadratic curve, which is due to the structure of the machine. In this case, the ripple is due to a jump in thread speed when an L3 or L4 cache is brought online due to increased socket and node counts. Here is the scaling profile for the first node, which contains one L4 cache and 34 cores:

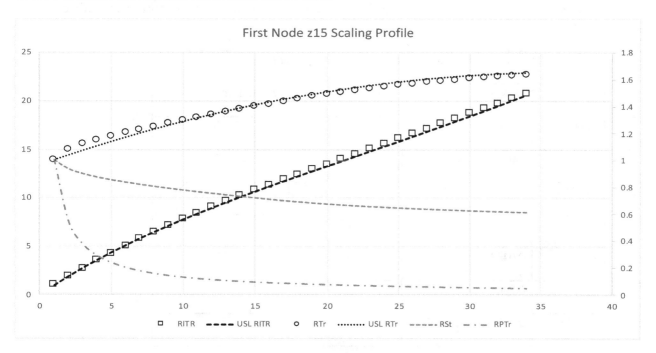

First Node z15 Scaling Profile

This chart includes the processor scaling USL models for RTr and RITR. The ripple effect of the nest structure (L3 caches) is apparent from the mismatch of the data with the model curves (dashed lines). Note that the RTr curve is convex, indicating negative kappa.

As the machine is scaled, it takes more work to fill up the caches leading to an element of Gustafson scaling. The ripples become more pronounced when the large L4 caches are added with nodes.

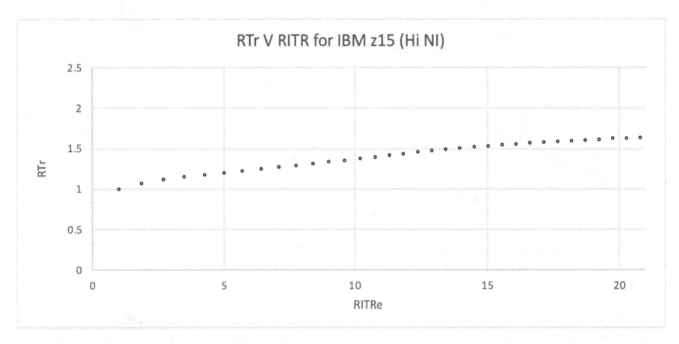

The chart above shows no nose, not even a knee. This is an indication that even at high scale, the workload is not overloading the machine. This is a further indication of Gustafson-like scaling. The USL model with negative kappa is a reasonable fit. It will take a piecewise model on a socket-by-socket (L3 by L3) basis to do better. Here is an historical perspective of the first node scaling for System z.

IBM System z USL Parameters for the First Node with Max RTr scale point					
	KAPPA	SIGMA	B	Cores/Node	Max RTr Cores
z9	-0.0018	0.0442	0.0424	8	10
z10	-0.0023	0.0627	0.0604	12	12
z196	-0.0016	0.0513	0.0497	15	14
z12EC	-0.0011	0.0473	0.0462	20	20
z13	-0.0007	0.0433	0.0426	30	29
z14	-0.0006	0.0403	0.0397	33	32
z15	-0.0005	0.0367	0.0362	34	35

Kappa has been approaching zero for at least seven generations of IBM zLSPR data. The Max RTr core count was always near the physical scaling limit of the machine.

IBM does not use the USL to design their machines or to create the high nest intensity ITR measurement loads that generated these results. However, being a vendor ITR measurement, both the design and the load have been optimized for over 50 years. This has pushed the results to the limits of both the scalability and this model.

Notice that kappa has been approaching zero over time, and sigma has been decreasing. Total cache has been increasing with each generation. The scaling of System z is approaching very good Amdahl scaling as the system evolves, even on this high nest intensity load.

PART 9: TANDEM OPERATIONS, TIERED SYSTEMS, AND ROUTINGS

So far, we have looked at the aggregate throughput of distributed hardware, but we have not looked at the performance of distributed systems that are operated one after another in tandem mode. The simplest tandem system is a routing in which there is a client computer and a host computer. Sometimes these are called a System of Engagement (SoE) and a System of Record (SoR).

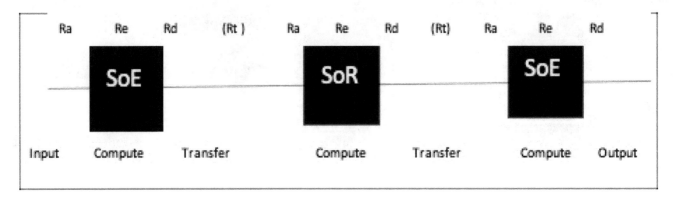

We will make the following simplifying assumptions.

1. The arrival rate Ra at the input will <= Rt.

2. All the compute execution rates are <= Rt.

3. Transfer rate on all lines is Rt.

This is essentially saying that the bottleneck rate Rb in one of the compute nodes is the transfer rate on the networks. We will also assume that the transfer time is essentially zero compared to the execution times in the compute nodes. This is not necessarily realistic, but it lets us consider the routing as having three rather than six stages.

You will also notice that we have two SoE stages in the routing. In reality, there is only one SoE, but there are input and output processes in that machine.

PARAMETERS FOR THE DIAGRAM ABOVE

The arrivals are exponentially distributed with Mean = 5.

The SoE Service Rate is normal with Mean 6 and Stdev 1.

The SoR Service Rate is normal with Mean 8 and Stdev 1.

In this type of operation, Tr for the "routing" is the sum of the individual stage response times. The ETR for the routing is the minimum of the individual stage ETRs. The average utilization of each stage is the arrival rate divided by the execution rate.

$$u = {R_a}/{R_s} = R_a T_s$$

Variability is also related to utilization:

When: $u \to 0$

$$c_d \to c_a$$

When: $u \to 1$

$$c_d \to c_s$$

We interpolate in the following way:

$$c_d{}^2 = u^2 c_s{}^2 + (1 - u^2) c_a{}^2$$

	EXPONENTIAL	NORMAL					
	RA	SoE Rs	SoE Rd	SoR Rs	SoR Rd	SoE Rs	SoE Rd
MEAN	5	6	5	8	5	6	5
STDEV	5	1	0.147	10	0.194	4	0.154
c	1	0.167	0.733	1.25	0.969	0.667	0.771
u		0.833		0.625		0.833	
c^2	1	0.028	0.537037	1.563	0.938	0.444	0.596
u^2		0.694		0.391		0.694	

Note that throughout the pipe, the mean arrival rate is five. However, the coefficient of variability, c, drops as the work traverses the pipeline, because $c_a > all\ c_s$. While this often happens, c can propagate through the pipe in any way according to this chart.

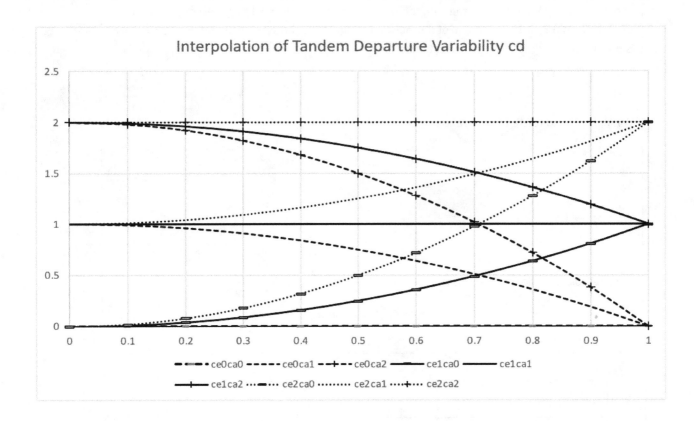

Interpolation of Tandem Departure Variability cd

Legend: ce0ca0, ce0ca1, ce0ca2, ce1ca0, ce1ca1, ce1ca2, ce2ca0, ce2ca1, ce2ca2

THE BOTTOM LINE ABOUT THE TANDEM OPERATION

Tandem operation increases response time and normalizes throughput to bottleneck service rate in the slowest stage. For each tier of the pipe:

$R_a , <= R_d , <= R_s$

The whole pipe is bottlenecked when one of the stages reaches 100% utilization and its $R_d = R_s$. The bottleneck rate is given by $R_B = R_s$ *of the slowest stage*. When an n stage pipeline is running at R_B:

$T_r >= sum(1/ s_i)$

That is, the response time is the sum of the service times unless a queue grows at the bottleneck because it is running at 100% utilization. This happens when Rd of the previous stage exceeds Rb. The variance of the rates within the pipeline will vary between the arrival and service variance of each stage, leading to the variability of the departure rate becoming a function of utilization.

PART 10: TRANSIENT BEHAVIOR

All of the propagation analysis of tandem systems above assumes that the pipeline operates in steady-state: That is, the initial conditions no longer affect the operation, the average queue length is short, and the pipeline is never empty. Analytic queueing models rarely "close" for transient conditions making the analysis complex. To understand transient behavior, it is often better to build a simulation model and run multiple scenarios on it, which has been done in a companion spreadsheet available to owners of this book. The spreadsheet is a simulation of a single server in which the arrival rate distribution is exponential and the service rate is constant.

The arrival data is derived from an exponential distribution with an average Ra = 5 (Stdev is also 5 because the distribution is exponential). This means that the variability of Ra is moderate. The ITR rate is assumed to be constant at the value put in the spreadsheet for the simulation run.

Here are the structure and formulas for the spreadsheet.

Input Variables						
		ITR	Ra			
Working Variables						
Interval	Random	Arrrivals	Queued	WIP	ETR	Response Time
i	Rand()	Round(-ln(Random(i)),0)	WIP(i-1)+Arrivals(i)	Arrivals(I) + Queued(i)	WIP(i)<=ITR,WIP(i),IT	WIP(i)/ITR
Results Variables						
		Arrivals/ITR	Queued/ITR	Response Time	Utiliation	
		Arrivals(i)/ITR	Queued(i)/ITR	WIP(i)/ITR	ETR(i)/ITR	

Here are the results of the runs with Ra = 5 ITR between 5 and 37.

ITR	Arrivals/ITR	Queued/ITR	WIP/ITR	Utilization	Avg Tr	Max Tr	ETR	Hravg
				Ra = 5, Umax =1				
5	0.9712	9.2756	10.2468	0.9364	88.7692	288	4.682	0.06791969
6	0.80933333	1.455	2.26433333	0.80566667	8.81733333	68	4.834	0.24120811
7	0.69371429	0.60257143	1.29628571	0.69257143	2.81428571	25	4.848	0.44389439
8	0.607	0.30525	0.91225	0.60625	1.665	19	4.85	0.64948454
9	0.53955556	0.17311111	0.71266667	0.53911111	0.99222222	14	4.852	0.85490519
10	0.4856	0.1052	0.5908	0.4854	0.7058	7	4.854	1.06015657
11	0.44145455	0.07109091	0.51254545	0.44145455	0.53781818	4	4.856	1.26523888
12	0.40466667	0.0505	0.45516667	0.40466667	0.4705	4	4.856	1.47116969
13	0.37353846	0.03692308	0.41046154	0.37353846	0.41953846	3	4.856	1.67710049
14	0.34685714	0.02771429	0.37457143	0.34685714	0.38171429	3	4.856	1.8830313
15	0.32373333	0.02053333	0.34426667	0.32373333	0.34853333	3	4.856	2.08896211
18	0.26977778	0.009	0.27877778	0.26977778	0.27977778	2	4.856	2.70675453
20	0.2428	0.0055	0.2483	0.2428	0.2492	2	4.856	3.11861614
25	0.19424	0.0016	0.19584	0.19424	0.19584	1.32	4.856	4.14827018
30	0.16186667	0.00066667	0.16253333	0.16186667	0.16253333	1	4.856	5.17792422
37	0.13124324	0	0.13124324	0.13124324	0.13124324	1	4.856	6.61943987

We want to specify the lowest ITR in which ETR and HR are high, Max Tr is tolerable, and Uavg is near or above 50%. The three gray horizontal rows are the most likely candidates. The gray shaded areas of ETR and HR show that ETR does not grow significantly for ITR>11, but the HR increases, diminishing the risk of being slammed by a black swan arrival event.

Here are some charts of this data.

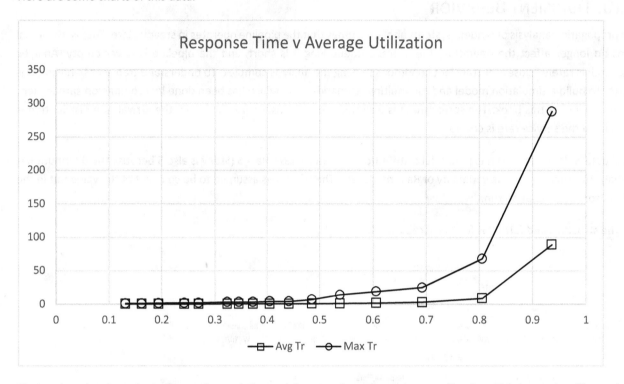

Notice that the shape is similar to the analytic model curve of response time v utilization. This is another illustration of the ETR/ITR duality principle. Keep in mind that the entire Max Tr curve occurs at cycles with u(t)=1.

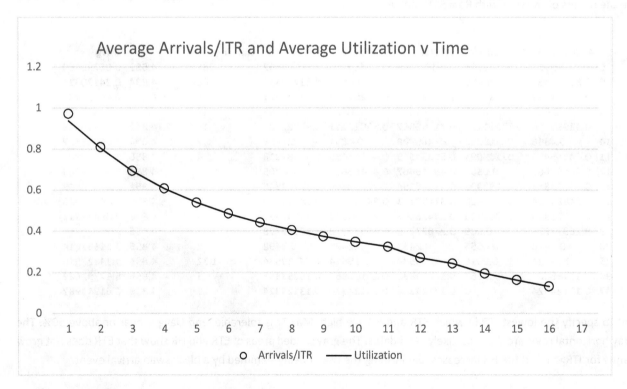

Notice that the average Arrivals/ITR tracks Uavg, which follows the assertion above about u= Ra/Rs. Consider transient behavior: peak Arrivals/ITR are > than 1. This means that there are arrivals greater than the ITR, indicating that arrivals will get queued at high traffic intervals. In the short term, queued arrivals spill over into subsequent cycles. The current cycle goes to u=1. Utilization for the cycles after the cycle at 100% have utilization greater than the arrival rate until the queue is exhausted or more arrivals are queued, keeping the utilization at 1. This is why the analysis of transient behavior is so complex. The spillover distorts short-term results while the transient occurs.

We will use ITR = 11 results for this in the following transient from the model:

Arrivals/ITR	Queued/ITR	Response Time	Utilization	HR	Arrivals/ITR-u
0.54545455	0	0.545454545	0.54545455	0.833333333	0
1.27272727	0	1.272727273	1	0	**0.272727273**
0.36363636	0.272727273	0.636363636	0.63636364	0.571428571	*-0.272727273*
0.18181818	0	0.181818182	0.18181818	4.5	0
1.18181818	0	1.181818182	1	0	**0.181818182**
0.27272727	0.181818182	0.454545455	0.45454545	1.2	*-0.181818182*
1.63636364	0	1.636363636	1	0	**0.636363636**
0.09090909	0.636363636	0.727272727	0.72727273	0.375	*-0.636363636*
0.09090909	0	0.090909091	0.09090909	10	0
0.54545455	0	0.545454545	0.54545455	0.833333333	0

Bold indicates a cycle where queueing occurs. HR = 0 and u = 1. Italics indicate cycles where spillover increases utilization. Here is the time series chart.

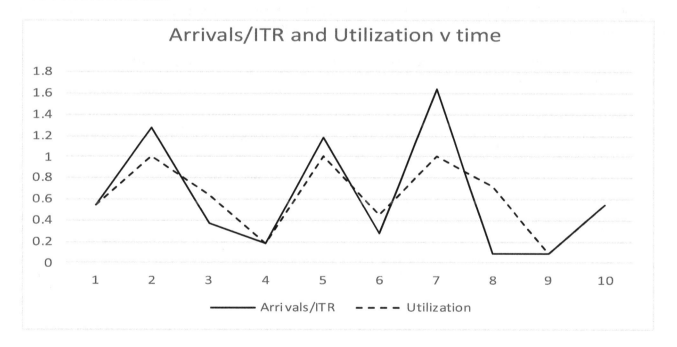

If ITR is increased, these transients will still be there, but the queueing decreases both in amount and frequency. If ITR is decreased, the queueing increases. Arrivals + Queueing is known as WIP (Work In Progress). If WIP/ITR > 1, utilization = 1. Otherwise, WIP/ITR = utilization.

Here are the time series distributions from the simulation run for ITR = 11 and Ra = 5:

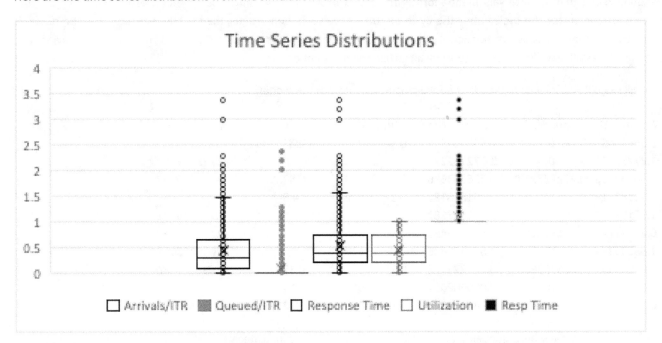

Notice that the distribution of utilization for the chosen optimization is at ITR = 11, the mean is at 50%, and the distribution of the tail is less fat and long. Also, c is significantly lower for the Rd than for Ra. You can see that using simulation to show the transient behavior has the added benefit of illustrating design tradeoffs.

This model can be extended for variable service time and multi-server solutions, but this is sufficient to demonstrate that spillover occurs in the transient case.

Part 11: A Workload Model

We started with scaling models and applied them to vendor data. We are now going to take a different approach and attempt to build a workload model that can be applied to various solution topologies and thread resources. The model needs the following elements:

1. Threads of work

2. Serial and parallel parts of work

3. Response Time Unit – threads used by a task

4. Cache required per thread

5. Usage pattern (peak and average) and service level

WE BUILD THE MODEL UPON THE IDEA OF A THREAD.

A workload consists of an aggregation of tasks that can run sequentially or in parallel. Each task consists of work that must be done sequentially and work that can be divided up and run in parallel. Tasks consist of threads that can be run in parallel up until the task requires a sequential operation. The extent to which threads can be run in parallel depends on both the ability of the task to spawn threads and the thread count provided by the system hardware and operating system. If either limit is surpassed, threads get "stacked" and run sequentially under the control of a scheduler. The tasks that we aggregate have a path length. Each has a serial part, which is run on one thread at a time. Each task has a parallel part that can be run on multiple threads at a time. Threads generated to run the parallel part are run sequentially if there are not enough available threads to run in parallel. Response Time Unit (RTU) sets the scalability of thread usage within a job, transaction, or query. A task will occupy up to RTU system threads. It will occupy RTU threads if:

1. Enough system threads are available

2. No thread interactions force threads to sleep

The hardware, software, or load can limit the parallelism achieved by the task. The behavior of the task itself will limit parallelism if the threads interact by communicating or sharing memory (or cache) locations.

There is one other limit to parallelism. Each thread of task contains work that must be completed sequentially and cannot be broken down into parallel threads. This is built into the thread itself. The amount of work required defines the "granularity" of the parallelism.

It can be advantageous to create RTU threads with path length L and run them in parallel. When s is small, each thread runs for T_t. As s gets larger, it becomes advantageous to use one thread for T = sL and RTU threads for T = (1-s)L/RTU. In this case, s must be large enough that the overhead of forking and joining the instruction streams (implies context switching) is small compared to the CPU resource "wasted" by running RTU threads for T = T_t. This occurs when the serial part is at the front and the back end of the execution rather than divided up into many small pieces.

A task with Path length = L contains a serial and a potentially parallel part.

$$L = sL + (1-s)L$$

This task can be split into a sequential part and a parallel part with path lengths:

$$L_s = sL$$

$$L_p = \frac{(1-s)L}{RTU}$$

This is Gustafson scaling expressed as time instead of speedup.

$$T_s = L_s$$

$$T_p = L_p$$

The time for the task is

$$T_t = L_s + L_p$$

$$T_t = sL + \frac{(1-s)L}{RTU}$$

The unit of L is cycles. These may be dispatch cycles or aggregated clock cycles. In the first case, the task will occupy RTU threads for L cycles. In the second case, a task will occupy RTU threads for (1-s)L cycles and one thread for sL additional cycles.

During that time the task will acquire and/or use cache space. Each thread will contend with other threads for shared cache space. In single-threaded cores, threads will dynamically contend for shared caches and sequentially contend for private cache space. On multithreaded cores, the threads will contend dynamically for private cache and for processor resources. We will need to apply a scaling model to account for access contention. We also must model cache occupancy by assuming some number of threads per MB of high-level cache. This will let us address the NI of the load. The first thing we must do is determine whether we are going to consider RTU to be one or greater than one. To do this we need to examine the data to see how it can be partitioned and then see how much work could run in each partition. The scaling model is also sensitive to thread interactions and bulk data traffic, which both contribute to nest intensity.

When we aggregate tasks into a workload, we will need to define a usage pattern to establish the queueing delays. This is done by defining the utilization of the peak and average values of the load. From this we can model HR; then if we define the service level k, we can model variability and UPI. Recall that **Upeak/Uavg = 1+kc**. We can either specify kmax and c or Upeak and Uavg to define a workload usage pattern. However, for realistic results, we should use existing usage patterns if they are available.

73

PART 12: SOME QUALITATIVE SCALING MODELS

We can also qualitatively evaluate workloads and fit them on various machine architectures and scaling models.

PFISTER'S PARADIGM

In his book *In Search of Clusters*, Dr. Gregory Pfister discusses how to exploit "clusters of small machines" by extracting the most parallelism possible from a workload.

SMP (multiple processors share a central memory), NUMA (multiple processors share memory, where each processor has a piece of memory that is local), cluster, and MPP (multiple processors that have private memories but a common "infrastructure") are all parallel systems of some sort. According to Dr. Pfister, four conditions are necessary for a workload to scale well on a parallel system:

1. Hardware that avoids serialization
2. The operating system avoids serial bottlenecks
3. The middleware avoids serial bottlenecks
4. The application avoids serial bottlenecks.

Hardware, OS, and middleware are usually designed for at least some degree of parallel operation. The application may or may not be designed for parallelism. Even when an application code avoids all unnecessary serialized implementation, the underlying business process or fundamental algorithm required by the application may not. As a result, some workloads are more suitable for parallelization than others. In other words, they scale differently because they have different levels of thread interaction, which is the source of serialization.

As the number of servers, nodes, or cores grows in a system, economics and physics dictate that they need to be smaller and less expensive. Here we define clusters as interconnected aggregations of small (but perhaps very fast) machines. Money is saved in the nest and I/O. Since some workloads cause more saturation than others, the effectiveness of the cluster solution will vary with the saturation on the servers configured. Nest Intensity (NI) of the load is a factor. Saturation at high utilization is almost always due to nest intensity.

Pfister combined these notions onto a chart that looks like this:

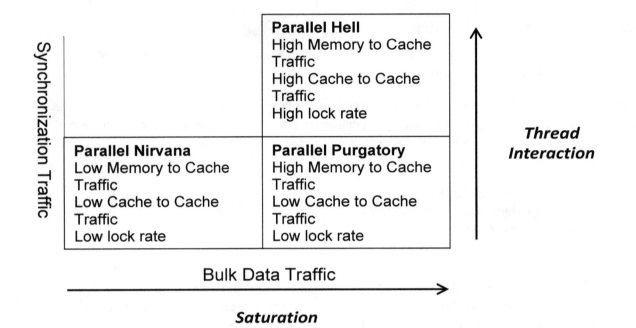

As bulk data traffic increases, so does NI. The arrow-labeled saturation is also a pointer to higher NI in the load. Pfister groups workloads by matching their behavior to the axes on this chart. For example, clusters of personal devices, clustered servers such as edge servers, and the IoT networks live in Parallel Nirvana. Data warehouses, business intelligence, and some decision support live in Parallel Purgatory. Highly scaled transaction processing, "mixed workloads," and high-density virtual machine environments live in Parallel Hell.

In shared memory infrastructures, bulk data traffic can lead to contention delays, causing saturation without any explicit thread interaction. The threads collide at the memory interface simply by attempting to access memory. The hardware makes the threads interact. This leads to contention delays even when there is no locking going on. The converse is also true. If there is thread interaction on an SMP, the data traffic increases. This is because in an SMP the locks are handled in memory, or at least in shared cache, causing L1 and L2 cache lines to be "cast out" and "migrated" or causing more "store through" traffic depending on the cache structure.

Data that is shared between threads must be moved to the cores running all the threads that share it. This explains the empty upper-left quadrant on Pfister's chart. It is very difficult to imagine a machine of any significant size in which there is thread interaction without a consequent increase in data traffic. By definition, very small single-threaded applications on dedicated hardware reside in the lower left quadrant near the origin. Examples are small personal, mobile, PoE, PoS, and IoT applications.

Pfister's Paradigm is useful for sorting workloads when we can characterize their bulk data and serialization traffic, as it is (thus far) impossible to optimize server design for more than one of the three regions on this chart. Pfister's chart can also be used to articulate trends: For example, there is a trend toward parallelization of codes. This means that new applications head toward Parallel Nirvana.

On the other hand, the current trend toward consolidation and virtualization is sending workloads toward Parallel Hell, as sharing resources drives more contention, and scheduling events cause more serialization delay and cache-to-cache traffic due to dispatching patterns.

It is difficult to quantify the vertical axis of Pfister's chart because there are so many different sources of serialization delay. However, it should be pretty clear that the right half of Pfister's space has high demand for memory and cache (high nest intensity). Low nest intensity workloads reside to the left of them.

GUNTHER'S PARADIGM

We have discussed Dr. Neil Gunther's two parameter (sigma and kappa) Universal Scaling Law. Sigma is a quantification of the contention delay, and kappa is a quantification of the coherency delay. Unfortunately, while this equation can be fit to scaling data, there is no way to precisely specify the parameters from a description of the application. Dr. Gunther has created a chart similar to the Pfister chart that lays out where workloads are expected to fall concerning the two parameters. We reproduce it here in a form that makes it easier to relate to Pfister's Paradigm[5].

	Class C Sigma = 0, Kappa >0 Scientific HPC computations On line Analytic Processing (OLAP) Data Mining Decision Support Software (DSS)	**Class D** Kappa and Sigma >0 Anything with Shared Writes Hotel Reservation System Banking OLTP Java Data Base Connectivity (JDBC)
Kappa (Coherence)	**Class A** Kappa and Sigma = 0 Shared nothing platform Google Text Search Lexus – Nexus Search Read only Queries	**Class B** Sigma > 0, Kappa 0 Message Based queueing (MQ Series) Message Passing Interface (MPI) applications Transaction Monitor (Tuxedo) Polling Service (VMware)

Sigma   (Contention)

---

[5] (Gunther) p 115

Class A applications are Parallel Nirvana applications if bulk data traffic is not too high. Class D is the same as Parallel Hell. Class B is pretty clearly Parallel Purgatory. On large servers, there is some contention for the shared memory and its nest but little or no thread interaction. Class C will not occur within a large server because the thread interaction caused by cache coherency traffic will generate contention. The workloads placed there by Gunther are often considered to be in Parallel Purgatory. OLAP is interesting if it shares data with an OLTP load. This adds contention to the load, which is often already in Parallel Hell.[6]

For class C, this situation can occur. Depending on the total traffic and the machine configuration, these loads can be viewed as in Parallel Nirvana, Parallel Purgatory, or Parallel Hell. On Pfister's chart, they can be located above and to the right of where clusters of blades want to be but below and to the left where it makes sense to run on large servers. Class C presents challenges to all platform types, but generally, the codes often run on MPPs and clusters quite well, indicating that in many cases the bulk data associated with the coherency traffic is not large.

There are applications for which the standard benchmarks will overestimate scaling as Gunther suggests in Chapter 8 of *Guerilla Capacity Planning.* It follows that the standard benchmarks will not produce valid metrics for class D workloads residing in Pfister's Parallel Hell.

---

[6] OLAP is On Line Analytic Processing and OLTP is On Line Transaction Processing. I once had a client who was adding real-time fraud detection to a critical transaction processing system that ran on an IBM mainframe. Their initial plan was to implement the solution on "commodity" distributed servers, but they were concerned about the increased response time. We recommended that they stay on the mainframe or use IBM's enterprise class Power servers. They chose to go to distributed Power servers and learned about Parallel Hell the hard way.

PART 13: WORKLOAD FIT: MODELING RELATIVE CAPACITY

We need a framework for studying machines as well as workloads.

MULTIDIMENSIONAL CAPACITY

If we relate our performance estimators to Pfister's paradigm:

Bulk Data Traffic → C_N (Nest Capacity)

Serialization Traffic → S_t (Thread Speed)

Parallelism → Threads (Core and/or Thread Count)

Positioning Machines by Workload Fit

We can get enough from the vendor websites to estimate N and S_t. In the following example we compare Intel Platinum Scalable to the IBM z14. Here is a summary of the data that we will use.

	Intel 8081 Platinum	IBM Z14	
Cores / Socket	28	6	
Threads / Core	1	1	Thread Count ignores SMT
Clock	2.9	5.5	Clock Rates estimate St
L3 / Socket	38.5	128	
L4 / Node	0	635	
Max Cache	308	2540	Cn
Nodes	1	4	
Sockets/Node	8	6	

We summarize this as follows:

Performance Indicator	Intel Platinum Scalable	IBM z14
C_N	308	2540
St	2.9	5.2
Threads	224	141

After normalizing the values so that the max machine has a score of 1 on each parameter, the results are displayed graphically to establish an initial positioning.

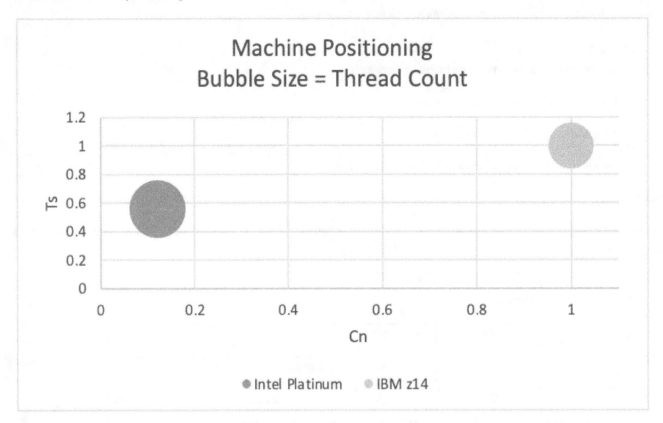

This chart shows the data in three dimensions by using bubble size to represent thread count. You can see that z14 has both the best estimated thread speed (S_t) and the largest cache (C_N). Intel has the most threads.

A Two-Dimensional View of Performance

Here we consider capacity to be two-dimensional. The two dimensions are throughput and capacity.

We have shown that:

$1/S_T >= T_r >= 1/ITR$

We have metrics and estimators for ITR and thread speed. We need to represent that ability to "stack" software threads on hardware threads. This is done with thread capacity.

$C_T = S_T\ C_N/Threads$

Both thread speed and C_N improve thread capacity. We divide C_N by threads to get the share of C_N that belongs to each thread in a fair division of resources. Since S_t = ITR/Threads, we also have:

$C_T = C_N ITR/Threads^2$

You can see here why the IBM Z system, which must handle high NI workloads, sacrifices processor socket space for L4 cache space. When T_r approaches $1/S_t$, extra threads can be a liability.

Here we plot normalized ITR V C_t :

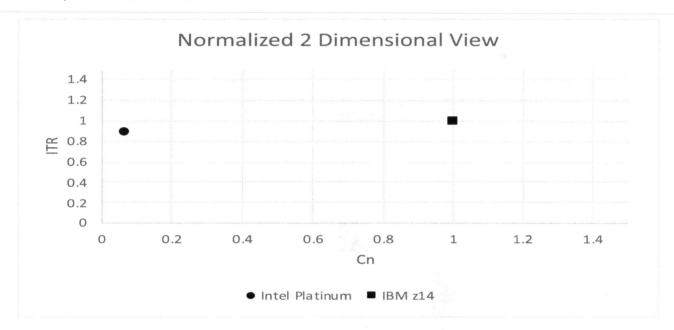

This chart shows the danger of using ITR as the sole performance metric. Thread capacity creates large Intel/IBM core ratios for workloads with significant thread stacking. Multi-tenant loads with a large number of users or virtual machines typically stack threads.

Thread capacity is also an indicator of a robust nest, which reduces NI effects. This is why the IBM mainframe remains entrenched in large enterprises. It is also why IBM did not use its Z processor for parallel supercomputers. High thread capacity also benefits workloads in which users experience response times that approach $1/S_t$ even if many concurrent threads run in parallel. Server chips of any kind are not used in cell phones or the Internet of things. There is no room or power for server chips. IoT and mobile devices do not benefit from either large C_N or thread count. Lack of a robust nes is why we won't see a surge of ARM-based servers unless a version of the architecture with large C_N evolves. Note that z14 has almost no ITR leverage on this estimate, but the C_t leverage is about an order of magnitude.

In the 1980s I asserted: "Processors are cheap; bandwidth is expensive. We make processors out of sand and recycled plumbing; connectors are gold-plated."

A colleague called this Temple's law. Another said, "Hogwash, you are not counting development." We were both right.

The "law" still applies today. Embedded processors are so inexpensive that we can use one to simply control an electric socket or lightbulb. Such devices consist of a processor core, a Wi-Fi network connection, some memory, and an actuator that flips a switch. There are more embedded processors than there are people.

On the other hand, a relatively low number of processors are found in mainframes, enterprise distributed servers, and supercomputers. These are very costly indeed. Only large businesses and institutions can afford them. The hardware difference is in the bandwidth per processor. This comes in the form of complex nests of switches and caches, robust I/O connections, multiple high-speed internal connections, and multiple large memory banks. Smaller distributed servers, point of engagement, personal, and mobile computers fall in between.

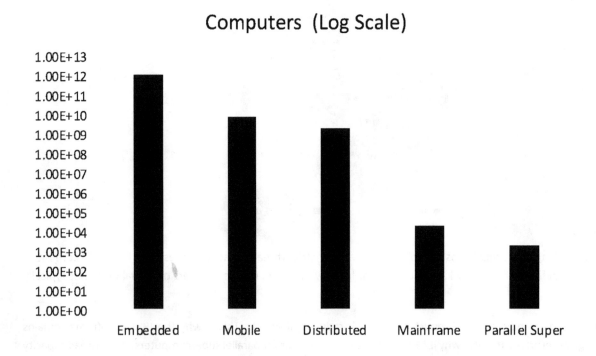

Pay attention to the logarithmic scale. Each "tic" on the axis is an order of magnitude of volume.

PART 14: PERFORMANCE ARCHITECTURE TOOLS

A great deal of performance work is done on existing solutions and machines. This is because we can't measure the solution designs. However, we can model them and measure the performance of prototyped solution elements. By making assumptions and approximations, we can establish a framework for guiding the solution design toward acceptable performance. This is aided by the fact that the hardware/operating system platform is typically chosen from preexisting alternatives. The solution performance design becomes a matter of platform selection rather than hardware design. We call the process "Performance Architecture." It is an amalgamation of Solution Architecture, Performance Engineering, and IT Infrastructure Design.

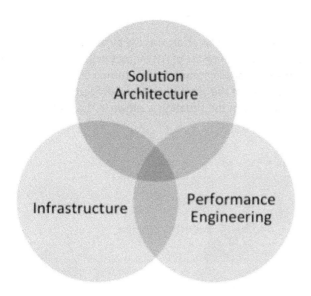

Performance Architecture

A PERFORMANCE ARCHITECTURE FRAMEWORK

This is the framework that was associated with my consulting business, Low Country North Shore Consulting, LLC. I am no longer holding it as proprietary because I am no longer consulting full time. The value of the methods is enhanced by publication. Here is the diagram of the framework:

THE FRAMEWORK IS A SET OF METHODS

Methods generate architecture work products. Work Products are typically graphic representations for design characteristics but can be tables or lists of specifications. Performance architecture work products quantify and display machine positioning, workload fit, and sizings. The objective of building the products is to provide performance guidance and insight to IT solution designers and architects.

The work products are also useful as collateral. They can be used to support business decisions, IT solution sales and marketing, IT infrastructure product pricing, and competitive analysis.[7] The framework is laid out sequentially. There is a natural progression in their usefulness, and the ability to generate them follows the solution design process.

THE DRIVING ISSUE

As we stated above, most solution design performance decisions are design decisions involving the mirror image twins Platform Selection and Workload Placement. Platform Selection is about specifying the type and model, and Workload Placement is about placing work on existing infrastructure. This involves multidimensional trade-offs. The task becomes very complex when we compare machine specifications.

One way the industry attempted to deal with this was to seek a common metric. This effort was led by vendors for whom performance was seen through the lens of ITR measurements. Recall the rather long list of ITR metrics in Section 1. Many of these had been built or proposed as common metrics for at least some class of programming. This turned out to be a fool's errand. These metrics sometimes work for comparing old and new machines of the same type. Many of them do not offer very much more insight than our clock times cores estimator. The complexity of the situation is shown in the graphic below.

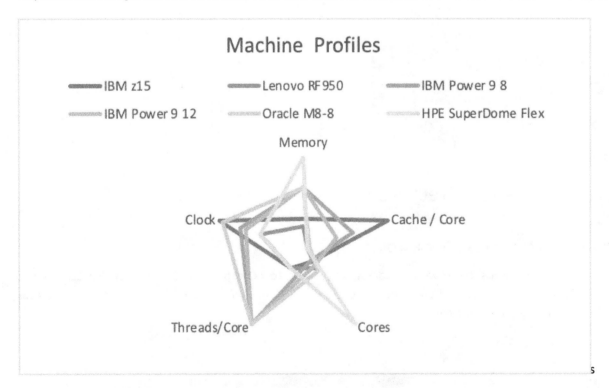

---

[7] One of the most fascinating aspects of all of this is that understanding and skills in the analysis of performance can get you involved in the technical aspects of many parts of a business or institution. My performance journey took me into development, sales, marketing, pricing, litigation, research, manufacturing, and intellectual property.

Multidimensional complexity leads to the desire to find a common metric.

It also thwarts the effort to apply the metric broadly with useful precision.

POSITIONING

ITR metrics are developed by benchmark measurements. The problem is that they measure ITR for some chosen standard of workload characteristics concerning nest intensity and I/O. That is, the precision of the benchmark depends on how close the workload's I/O, memory, and cache requirements are to the benchmarks' reliance on those resources. It is desirable to make the design ratio of Throughput/Capacity (aka E/B[8]) apparent in a comparison of machines. This is what positioning does.

The positioning process has four steps:

> Gather Published Specifications (Cores, Threads, Clock, Cache)

> Calculate Throughput and Capacity

> Calculate Design Ratios

> Plot Results for Analysis

We know how to estimate throughput from machine specifications:

ITR = Clock Speed x Cores x Threading Improvement

And we can estimate capacity as:

C_t ~ Total High-Level Cache x Thread Speed

---

[8] E/B is a very old term for the design ratio expressed as Execution/Bandwidth.

Here is a table of specifications for a set of Enterprise-Class Servers plus the IBM z15 Mainframe.

	Machine SPECs and Model					
	IBM z15	Lenovo RF95	IBM Power 9	IBM Power 9	Oracle M8-8	HPE SuperDome Flex
Installed Cor	240	224	128	192	256	896
System Core	20	0	0	0	0	0
Spare Cores	2	0	0	0	0	0
Dead Cores	28	0	0	0	0	0
CP Cores	190	224	128	192	256	896
Cores/Socket	11.875	28	8	12	32	28
Threads/Core	2	2	8	8	8	2
Sockets/Nod	4	4	4	4	8	4
Nodes/Mach	4	2	4	4	1	8
Clock	5.2	2.7	3.95	3.7	5	2.7
Turbo	5.2	4	4	3.9	5	3.9
L1I/Core	0.125	0.0312	0.0625	0.0625	0.0625	0.0312
L1D/Core	0.125	0.0312	0.0625	0.0625	0.03125	0.0312
L2I/Core	4	1	0.5	0.5	0.25	1
L2/Core	2				0.125	
L3/Socket	256	35.5	120	120	64	35.5
L4/Node Sha	980					
L4/Socket at memory			128	128		
Memory TB	32	24	64	64	64	96
Cache / Core	20.6315789	1.26785714	16	10.6666667	2	1.267857143
Core increm	1	28	4	4	32	28
Scaling Parm	1	1	1	1	1	1
ITR/Core						
Core ITR						
SMT	IBM z15	Lenovo RF95	IBM Power 9	IBM Power 9	Oracle M8-8	HPE SuperDome Flex
1	5.2	2.7	3.95	3.7	5	2.7
2	6.76	3.51	6.715	6.29	6.5	3.51
4			9.2825	8.695	9	
8			11.692	18.6184	11	
Thread Speed						
	IBM z15	Lenovo RF95	IBM Power 9	IBM Power 9	Oracle M8-8	HPE SuperDome Flex
1	5.2	2.7	3.95	3.7	5	2.7
2	3.38	1.755	3.3575	3.145	3.25	1.755
4			2.320625	2.17375	2.25	
8			1.4615	2.3273	1.375	

All of these machines can run more than one core per thread, so clock x cores ITR has to be refined by an SMT thread speed estimate. To facilitate this, the table includes entries for ITR/Core and Thread speed variation by thread count for each machine.

From these take thread count, total cache, and thread speed and put them into another table that includes estimates for capacity and throughput calculated from the specifications. We then normalize so that the value of the largest value column is 1.

	Threads	Cache	Thread Speed		Capacity Cache x Ts	Throughput ITR
z15	0.07080078	1	1		1	0.23974868
	0.14160156	1	0.65		0.65	0.31167328
Lenovo	0.109375	0.07244898	0.51923077		0.03761774	0.19230769
	0.21875	0.07244898	0.3375		0.02445153	0.25
IBM p9 12	0.09375	0.52244898	0.68269231		0.3566719	0.21672772
	0.1875	0.52244898	0.47788462		0.24967033	0.3034188
	0.375	0.52244898	0.34134615		0.17833595	0.43345543
	0.75	0.52244898	0.20480769		0.10700157	0.52014652
IBM p9 24	0.1875	0.52244898	0.68269231		0.3566719	0.43345543
	0.375	0.52244898	0.47788462		0.24967033	0.60683761
	0.75	0.52244898	0.34134615		0.17833595	0.86691087
ORACLE M8	0.125	0.130612245	0.96153846		0.1255887	0.40700041
	0.25	0.130612245	0.625		0.08163265	0.52910053
	0.5	0.130612245	0.43269231		0.05651491	0.73260073
	1	0.130612245	0.26442308		0.03453689	0.8954009
HPE Superdone Flex	0.4375	0.289795918	0.51923077		0.15047096	0.76923077
	0.875	0.289795918	0.3375		0.09780612	1

This is the data that we will use to create three work products that can be used to position the machines on performance.

1. Analysis 1 shows a scatter graph of throughput v capacity broken into quadrants.

2. Analysis 2 show the same scatter graph with a line for throughput = capacity that divides the designs between throughput biased and capacity biased machines.

3. Analysis 3 shows the design ratio for each point on the graph, allowing us to quantify the amount of bias.

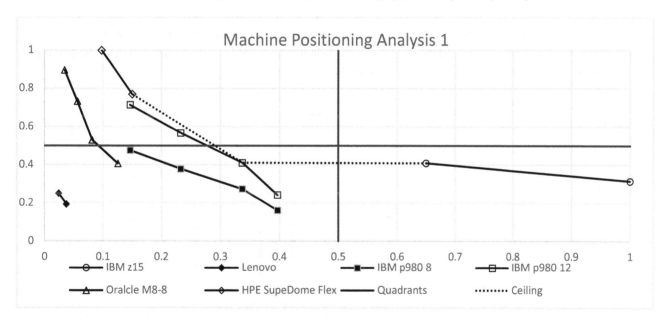

The first thing to see from this chart is that there is no machine in the upper right quadrant. This indicates a design trade-off between throughput and capacity. That is, the machines in the upper left (Enterprise Distributed Servers) trade off capacity for throughput, and the mainframe trades off throughput for capacity. The machines in the lower left compete on cost/performance.

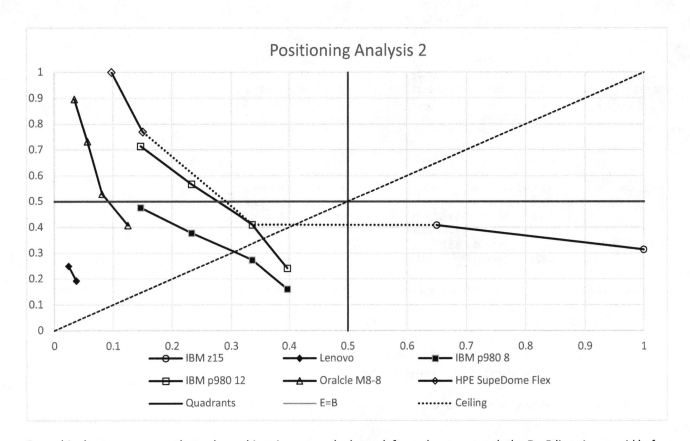

From this chart, you can see that only machines in or near the lower left quadrant approach the E = B line. As we said before, machines above the line are throughput biased, and those well below the line are capacity biased. It is useful to quantify the design ratio for each machine. This is shown in the bar chart below.

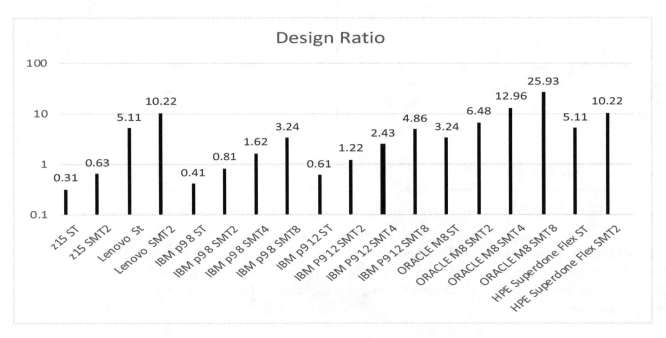

WORKLOAD FIT POSITIONING

In the discussion of positioning, we only considered the hardware specification of the machines that are platform candidates. We developed and quantified the notion of the E/B Design Ratio and quantified it for a set of machines. Since our objective is to specify machines to place work on existing infrastructure with an optimal "workload fit," we must consider the workload characteristics concerning throughput, capacity, and E/B requirements to determine the workload fit.

We do this by comparing the E/B requirements ratio to the E/B design ratios of the candidate machines. A simple comparison of the requirements ratio to various design ratios can determine the best-fit machines to use. When the design ratio is larger than the requirements ratio, there will be an abundance of throughput when the capacity requirement is met. If the design ratio is smaller than the requirements ratio, capacity will be abundant when the throughput requirement is met.

This can be done on the same graph as the positioning work by adding a line whose slope is the requirements ratio. Here the workload ratio is set to 1.5.

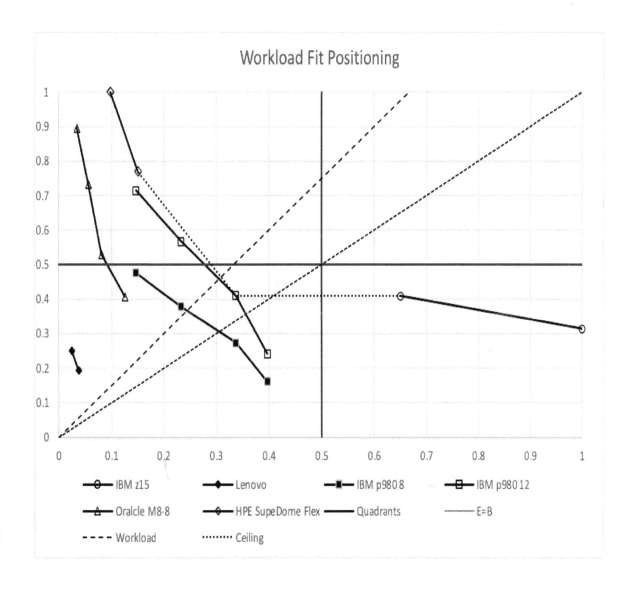

Notice that the workload ratio needs to be extreme to perfectly fit the more extreme design ratios. On the other hand, moderate design ratios will only fit "smaller" machines in the lower left quadrant. Workloads that require both high bandwidth and high capacity fall into the upper right quadrant of the graph, where there are no machines. This does not mean that there is no solution. It means that the workload needs to be partitioned onto multiple nodes. These can take the form of a cluster of machines that reside in the lower left quadrant or the form of a "Parallel Supercomputer." For extremely high workload ratios, the workloads will fit on the machines in the upper left quadrant. Very low workload ratios result when multiple workloads share a single machine. This is what the mainframe does uniquely well. Some will argue that the machines in the upper left can consolidate workloads, but typically this is more an exercise in partitioning than actually sharing resources. However, the higher capacity machines in the lower left quadrant can accomplish the same thing on fewer resources.

Taken by volume, most computers (Embedded Mobile and Personal Distributed computers) reside near the origin of this graph. The work placed there is highly localized in nature and typically is limited both by the nature of the work and by the resources available to be relatively low throughput and capacity in nature.

It should be apparent that a personal device cannot possibly hold all the information to do the work the user needs to be done. Similarly, a personal device is not going to do things like predicting the weather. Performance Architecture provides the metrics and methods by which we make the design decisions about where work gets done in an IT infrastructure. It is also about making design choices for the infrastructure elements that supply the needed throughput and capacity.

It is useful to quantify workload fit. We do this by dividing the design ratio by the workload ratio and comparing the result to a perfect fit where the result is one.

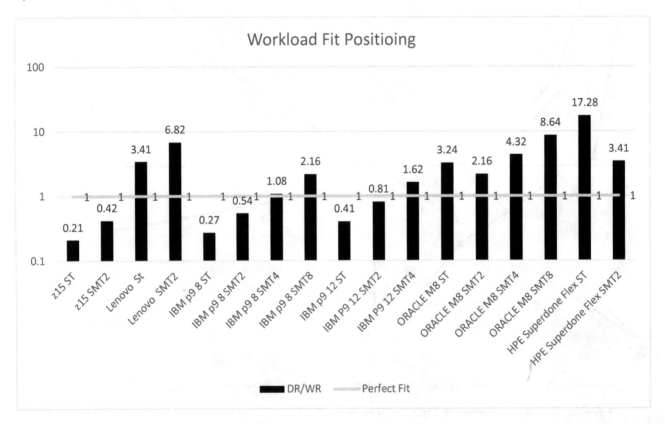

For DR/WR > 1 there will be an abundance of throughput when the capacity requirement is met. For DR/WR>>1, this becomes expensive. For DR/WR <1 capacity will be abundant when the throughput requirement is met. For DR/WR<<1 this also gets expensive.[9] In this case, the IBM p980 with eight cores per socket appears to be the closest fit.

COMPUTER TAXONOMY AND DESIGN RATIOS

Computer	Sub Class	Design Ratio
Embedded		High
Mobile	Auto	High
	Phone	
	Tablet	
Distributed	Personal	High
	Local	
	Data Center	Moderate
Mainframe		Low
	IBM z	
Super	Data Intense	Moderate
	Compute Intense	High

POSITIONAL SIZING

A positional sizing provides an estimate of the relative performance of a solution on a set of machines, given some basic workload characteristics. The workload is defined by the parameters kmax and c. We define the machine with the smallest capacity to contain the load. We then determine how many loads the others can consolidate based on their capacity. From this, we determine the average utilization of the consolidated loads and generate ETR and UPI values. We normalize ITR, ETR, UPI, and capacity and plot them on radar charts. A wider diamond indicates larger ETR and ITR. A taller diamond indicates higher capacity and better UPI (translates to response time). Because of SMT, we plot two charts.

---

[9] This is a simplification. Each of the machines on this version of the chart is a fully populated maximum version of the machine represented. From this starting point we can look for more precisely matching requirements by exploring specific model configurations.

Here are the results for k = 5 and c =1:

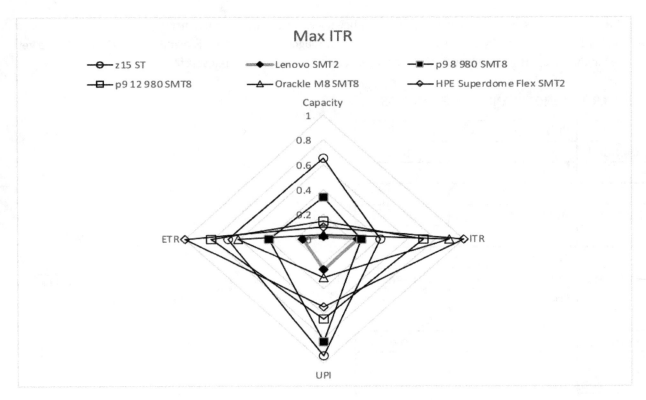

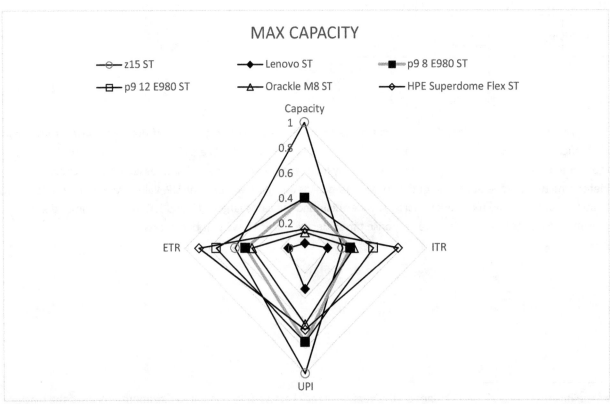

The parameters k and c have no impact on the capacity and ITR values for the machines. However, increasing either will push the ETR toward the center. Increasing c will push UPI toward the center. Similarly, decreasing either will move ETR toward ITR, and decreasing c will move UPI toward 1 (the maximum).

The shapes of these profiles will point to throughput v capacity bias of the machines and also indicate their design ratios. Wide diamonds have high design ratios and are throughput biased. Tall diamonds have low design ratios and are capacity biased. The advantage of this work product is that it takes into account all three views of performance plus capacity.

ITR → Vendor View

ETR → Owner View

UPI → User View

C_n → Capacity

To include the User View without having UPI would require us to know a great deal more about the workload and machines.

A KEY DESIGN QUESTION

"Are your design requirements throughput- or capacity-oriented?"

While we need to know quite a bit about the workload to determine the workload ratio, we should have some idea about the workload bias based on the type of application that we are building. The following guidelines, which help determine the bias early in the game, are based on experience.

The workload is Throughput-Oriented if:

- The load consists of a few major elements

- Individual load elements can use many threads in parallel

- Response time unit of work consists of the work of many threads

- There are relatively few users

- The expected usage pattern will efficiently utilize a significant portion of the allocated resources

- The expected usage pattern will have relatively low variability

Also:

- CPU intense loads are more throughput-oriented than data-intense loads.

- Analytic or query loads can be more throughput-oriented than transactional loads.

- Throughput-oriented loads have an affinity for partitioned and dedicated resources but can share resources in coarse-grained consolidations.

The workload is Capacity-Oriented if:

- The load consists of many small elements

- Each element uses a single or small number of threads

- The response time unit of work consists of a single thread or a small number of parallel threads

- There are relatively many users

- The load will gain efficiency in using resources by aggregation of user loads or consolidation with other loads

- The individual usage patterns will have high variability

- Data intense loads are more capacity-oriented than CPU intense loads of similar structure

- Transactional loads are more capacity-oriented than analytic or query loads

- Capacity-orientated loads have an affinity for multi-tenancy and fine-grained consolidation

CORE RATIO SIZINGS

Typically, we are trying to determine how many cores of a given type we need to do the job at hand. There are four kinds of sizings that we can do once we have sufficient data.

1. Benchmark-based sizing

2. Measurement plus

3. Workload type with usage pattern input

4. Consolidation/distribution sizing

BENCHMARK-BASED SIZINGS

On the surface, this looks like an improvement over our clock x cores with SMT modifier modeling. In particular benchmark results can:

1. Account for processor design and compiler differences

2. Account for OS overhead differences

3. Take scaling into account if multiple instances of scale are measured

However, creating a benchmark that is both representative and economical to run can be a very time- and resource-intense undertaking. As a result, people often look for common metrics, usually from industry-standard or middleware benchmarks, to stand in for a custom effort. The problem then becomes a matter of coverage and fit for the situation at hand. Over time given evolutionary platform changes, it is possible to develop sizing methodologies using vendor metrics like IBM's LSPR and rPerfs, third-party metrics like RPEs, or middleware metrics like SAPs or the SAP Hanna benchmark. These can work quite well if you are not considering platform changes either onto or off of the platform that you have experience with. Indeed, even MHz will work within an Intel environment.

WORKLOAD TYPE PLUS USAGE SIZINGS

When considering replacement platforms either for distribution or consolidation of work, this method of sizing is often useful. It is based on creating a core ratio between the old and new machines. In this method, the practitioner decides the category of work to which the application belongs. A workload factor and a utilization factor are applied. The workload factor is based on previous experience and scales the core rate up or down away from the "a core is a core" clock times cores model. Then a utilization factor is applied when the new machine is expected to tolerate a different Umax or Uavg than the old machine. This type of sizing originated at IBM in the 1990s to provide reasonable guidance to clients who were moving work onto the mainframe through consolidation or off it due to distribution. The downside of this method is that it takes a long time to build up the knowledge of workload factors from experience, benchmarks, and other measurements.

MEASUREMENT PLUS SIZINGS

Dr. Richard Hamming[10] advocated a bottom-up approach to programming the critical path of an application, because it leads to early prototype code for use in modeling and measuring performance. The measurement plus sizing method is based on the availability of such prototype code. The idea is that we measure the prototype code on platforms of interest to determine thread speed, RTU, and scaling. If at all possible, we should also measure cache usage, though this is rarely done. Such measurements can give us an idea of the workload bias and how the available platforms react to the code.

You may have noticed the speed or scaling factor rows in the spreadsheet matrices we used for positioning. These are put there to allow modification of the basic specifications, based on measurements. Typically, these measurements are not as extensive as common benchmarks. They can lead to an earlier and better understanding of platform options. Also, they can be used much earlier in the design process

CONSOLIDATION DISTRIBUTION SIZINGS

This type of sizing uses measured usage patterns to determine the impact of removing or adding load to a system. The function by which the utilization is turned into an ITR can be anything from clock x cores to benchmark results to measured production data. The point is that the sizing is driven by actually measured production utilization of the load components. The consolidation study done earlier in this book was a consolidation distribution sizing.

---

[10] (Hamm) Dr. Hamming mentions this in several places and contexts in his book.

SIZING CONCLUSIONS

Regardless of the type of sizing done, certain principles remain the same.

Precision will be limited by the resources and time available.

A sizing is not a capacity plan, which can only be done based on measured production rates.

The time and resources put into sizings should expand as the design progresses.

Over-investment in sizings is a waste of resources and may delay results.

Underinvestment in sizings leads to unpleasant surprises in production.

The development process has an impact on how soon this can be done, the efficacy of the results, and the cost to perform the work.

It is worth paying attention to Dr. Hamming's assertion that the critical path should be *designed* and coded from the bottom up.

APPENDIX A. METHOD FOR REGRESSION OF SCALING MODELS

DR. GUNTHER'S METHOD FROM HIS BOOK *GUERILLA CAPACITY PLANNING*[11]

Gunther defines the Deviation from Linear (DFL)

DFL(n) = RTr(n)-1

The method uses a transformation of variables X = n-1 to get a quadratic regression equation:

DFL(x) = AX^2 + BX

Regression is done on the data pairs (n-1), RTr(X) -1

We have shown the algebra that transforms A and B into the kappa and sigma parameters of the USL. The regression can be done using regression software such as is found in the "R Suite" or other statistical programming toolsets. Gunther also suggests that this form can be regressed using an Excel x – y scatter graph and setting a polynomial trend line of order 2 with an intercept of zero. The displayed equation will supply A and B. We have shown that we can do the same thing directly on:

RTr(n) = A(n-1)^2 + B(n-1) +1

This regression can be done by plotting RTR(n) v (n-1) and setting the intercept to 1 for the trendline. This will result in the same regression coefficients and USL model parameters.

---

[11] (Gunth) Chapter 5 pp. 75-79

APPENDIX B: THE LAWS OF IT PHYSICS

This is a paraphrase of "The Laws of Factory Physics."[12] I am supplying this because it provides English statements for a lot of the math in this book. Some will find it helpful when the math looks like gibberish. However, since performance is essentially a quantification, a certain amount of math is required as you will see in the "Laws" below.

LAW 1 – LITTLE'S LAW: INTRINSIC THROUGHPUT RATE

Throughput is work divided by time. In a computer, this is most simply put as "instructions per second." In transferring data over a network, bus, or channel between storage devices, this is most simply put as "bits per second." In general, the throughput of IT solutions is expressed as "units of work per second." Units of work could be Jobs, Programs, Program Steps, Dialog Steps, Transactions, Queries, Floating Point Operations, etc. Since there are many different types of work, there are many different metrics that take the form:

> Throughput Rate = Work Units / Time

If we define the Work Unit is as work done by one thread and Time as the time to complete work on a single thread, and we invert Time into speed, we get:

> ITR = Threads x Thread Speed

This is Little's Law of Throughput.

(The Vendors' law)

LAW 2 – BEST-CASE PERFORMANCE

If the thread speed remains constant at S0, then we achieve maximum best-case performance.

> If Software Threads <= Hardware Threads, ITR = Software Threads x S0

> Otherwise, ITR = Hardware Threads x S0

LAW 3 – WORST-CASE PERFORMANCE

If thread speed remains constant at S0 and there is one software thread, then ITR = S0.

LAW 4 – MALLEABILITY OF INFORMATION

In Factory Physics, materials are conserved. That is, the materials in = materials out - waste + any parts produced in the process. However, information is created from copies of data by IT systems. Even if the programs leave the copy intact in memory, there is no reason to restore it by sending it back to storage when the program is done with it. The copy is overlaid with a copy of new data when the old data is no longer required. The data out is usually proportional to the data in but is scaled up or down by processing. The process either summarizes the data or expands it by generating new information. Thus, data out can be greater than or less than data in.

---

[12] (Hopp) pp. 622-624

Law 5 – Effective Transaction Rate (ETR)

In general, an IT system will have an average ETR that is strictly less than the rated ITR.

$$ETR_{avg} < ITR$$

(The Owners' law)

Law 6 – Variability

Increasing variability always increases Response Time, reduces average utilization, and increases the required headroom (HR).

Law 7 – Variability Placement

Variability at the front end (engagement or edge tier) of a solution has a larger impact than in the back end (data tier). The impact on the logic tiers will fall in between.

Law 8 – Utilization

Increasing utilization without making other changes always increases response time in a highly nonlinear fashion.

8.1 Utilization is a statistic.

8.2 It is always a count of busy cycles/elapsed cycles.

8.3 At any cycle utilization is utilized units/configured units; where unit utilization is either 1 or 0.

8.4 As the measurement interval increases, the peaks and troughs approach the long-term average.

8.5 As the measurement interval decreases, the peaks and troughs approach 1 and 0 respectively.

8.6 For a sufficiently long period of consideration, the average remains constant.

8.7 Utilization is not a normal statistic; the tails are fat and possibly long. The distribution is typically skewed (the average is not the same as the median).

8.8 In IT systems utilization, capacity, and time are quantized.

Law 9 – Move Batches

In IT a "routing" is a combination of network hops and computing that is done at compute nodes. For any routing, the response time will be proportional to the size of the batches (packets) moved on the network.

LAW 10 – PROCESS BATCHES

In IT a unit of work is dependent on the work to be done. It could be work done by a single instruction, or the work done in a single clock cycle, or the work done in a single dispatch cycle, or the work done by a single instance of a program.

If there is significant setup time (loading the program and data into memory, connecting to users, allocating resources, and initially dispatching the program), then:

1. The minimum batch size that yields a stable system may be greater than one work unit.
2. As the number of units per batch increases, the batch response time grows proportionally to the batch size.
3. If setup times are long enough, there will be a batch size greater than one for which the response time is minimized.

LAW 11 – PAY ME NOW OR PAY ME LATER

If you cannot pay for variability reduction, you *will* pay in one or more of the following ways:

1. High response time with high queuing delays
2. Wasted resources (low utilization)
3. Lost throughput (ETR/ITR <<1)

LAW 12 – LEAD TIME

In a factory, the lead time includes order processing and delivery time in addition to the factory's cycle time to build the product. In IT we can think of the factory cycle time to run the backend logic and data handling and the lead time as the backend time plus the client processing and network delays outside of the data center.

Lead time is an increasing function of both the mean and variance of the entire routing.

LAW 13 – RESPONSE TIME

Response Time is the sum of queue time, process time, wait for batch time, move time, and sometimes wait for match time.

(The Users' Law)